Work With Who You Are

Published by Goosecreek Publishers, 9900 Corporate Campus Drive, Suite 3000, Louisville, Kentucky, 40223, (502) 657-6383, www.goosecreekpublishers.com.

For general information on our other products and services, please contact our Customer Care Department within the United States at (866) 986-2726, outside the United States at (502) 587-0331.

Library of Congress Cataloging-in-Publication Data

Brown, Denise.
    Work With Who You Are: Timely Direction to Reveal Your
    Natural Attractiveness

Designed by David Hartman Designs
Cover photography by Dean Lavenson Photography

ISBN 1-59633-005-8 $19.95

Printed in the United States of America

10 9 8 7 6 5 4 3 2 1

Work With Who You Are

Timely Direction to reveal your "Natural Attractiveness"

by Denise Brown

Acknowledgements

To my husband, Ronel, thank you for seeing God's plan for our lives and for your commitment to follow through on every detail.

To our children, BJ, Ahsha and Thobi, thank you for your patience and understanding during countless schedule changes.

To my Mom, thank you for being a living example of "nothing is too hard for God." During challenging times, your encouragement pointed me to God's path.

A Timely Direction Book ™

How To Use This Book

This book is designed to surface, challenge and change your underlying assumptions about you. Many variables impact our lives, yet none have any bearing on our inherent potential to accomplish great things. Use this book to clarify and redefine your capacity for greatness. You were uniquely created with everything you need to reach your full potential.

Believing you have everything you need is just the beginning. Using what you have is the next step. It's up to you to use what you have or waste your time trying to use someone else's gifts and live someone else's life.

"*Work With Who You Are*" is about making a conscious choice to use what's already available to you—to uncover the treasure locked within you and use it to propel you toward achieving your full potential. A life transformation is inevitable as you become more self aware and clear on your life's purpose.

"Life is a daring adventure or nothing at all," said Helen Keller. Even with its challenges, life is meant to be enjoyed, not endured. This book is about making the most of this life with the hand you've been dealt—it's exactly the hand you were supposed to get. How you respond to the hand you've been dealt makes all the difference in the world.

Table of Contents

Chapter One
Clearing the Decks

"Overloaded people fail"
—T.D. Jakes

Introduction

The most difficult step of any journey is the first step. First steps move you from comfort and familiarity to uncharted territory. Whether you take the first step is often the difference between greatness and mediocrity. Someone once said that " 90% of success is showing up everyday."

Getting started is like showing up—it is a voluntary choice and requires courage and persistence. Since you've decided to start your journey to pursue your dream, let's begin by clearing the space around you. Along the way, you will make many choices and decisions—some will accelerate your progress and others have the potential to derail your forward progress. Some decisions will require leaving activities or relationships behind.

More importantly, clutter is a reflection of what's going on inside—it reveals the heart of the matter.

Why start with clutter? Everyone can relate to having a clutter in their lives. It's such an innocent thing and is an accepted part of our culture. Rarely noticing its effects, we really don't believe clutter is a problem. Clutter is deceiving and revealing. It's deceiving because clutter is great camouflage for hiding areas in need of personal development. More importantly, clutter is a reflection of what's going on inside—it reveals the heart of the matter.

A stable lifestyle has as its foundation consistency and calmness. Clutter interferes with that foundation by disturbing order and tranquility. This chapter underscores the importance of clearing clutter and minimizing its negative impact. A frequent cause of premature derailments, we'll define clutter, discuss its consequences and identify strategies to remove it and maintain a clutter free environment.

Clearing the decks

Clearing your space to pursue your purpose is like a naval ship clearing its decks in preparation for battle. Since the smallest skirmish has the potential to result in the ship's destruction, no battle is taken lightly. An effective commander will spare no effort to ensure the ship's success in battle. Nothing is allowed to get in the way of the ship's most important weapon—the use of its guns. It's the commander's responsibility to clear the decks of anything that would impede the firing of the ship's guns. To do anything less would place the lives of the crew and the ultimate protection of the ship at risk.

Who you are includes your personal values, innate strengths and talents and your spiritual foundation.

Your most important endeavor is to understand your life's purpose and pursue it. It is just as important to you as the ship's guns are in battle. And just like the commander, you need to clear your decks to gain a clearer picture of who you are and what's important to you. Knowing who you are is the most important calling of your life and it is the key to reaching your full potential. Who you are includes your personal values, innate strengths and talents and your spiritual foundation.

Who you are is more than the work you do everyday or what possessions you own. Defining who you are started the day you were born and continues throughout your lifetime.

Along life's journey, many experiences add to that definition and when they have served their useful purpose or become baggage, those experiences should be discarded. Clear everything from your decks that has the potential to hold you back from reaching your full potential.

Taking time to clear the space before the journey will help you make decisions that are "right for you" and result in discovering your life purpose. Remove anything that obscures your ability to see your future or hinders your self awareness. In other words, traveling light for the journey is a prerequisite for success on the journey. Clutter obstructs vision and hides your natural attractiveness. An old proverb says it like this, "the way of a fool seems right in his own eyes." (Proverbs 12: 15) In other words, when your focus is not clear, a bad choice can seem like a right choice.

Clutter can appear in your mental and emotional space, in your financial, relational and wellness space.

Clutter easily obscures your vision and leads to poor decisions and results. In hindsight, you find that your choices would have been quite different if you could have cleared the decks before the decision. Clutter is an impediment to your creativity, productivity and your ability to work with who you are achieve your goals.

What is clutter?

Macmillan's Children's Dictionary describes clutter as "a messy collection of things." Webster's defines it as "a crowded or confused mass of things." Clutter is anything that you don't use or need and it goes beyond your physical living environment. Clutter can appear in your mental and emotional space and in your financial, relational and wellness space. Even poor time management is a result of clutter.

It's unfinished business and unresolved questions or decisions. Clutter is anything that requires more of your time and attention than what it is worth and has no practical benefit. That includes activities, people and work that don't consistently enhance the quality of your life. If you're beginning to feel surrounded by clutter, you're getting the picture.

How does clutter impact you?

Clutter chaos drains energy, robs creativity, reduces focus and controls you. I realize that sounds like a very tall order for such a small thing, however, studies have shown that clutter impacts you by diverting your focus and attention. No matter the role, clutter diminishes your effectiveness and is a distraction.

Clutter interferes by obscuring vision and draining your energy with constant negative mental chatter. It always starts out as a small problem that takes on more significance as we allow it to expand. It has the ability to change the direction of your life because it can impact so many areas. As a coach, I've spoken with individuals who were literally paralyzed by the clutter in their lives. The prospect of decluttering overwhelmed them. As a matter of fact, many have lived with the clutter so long, they believe it must be a way of life for them.

Clutter chaos drains energy, robs creativity, reduces focus and controls you.

Everyone can relate to the lightened load and sense of freedom you experience when everything has a place and is in its place. I was amazed at the new energy I felt when I decluttered the storage areas in my home. It felt and looked so good, I would open the door just to look at the nice, organized, uncluttered space. It motivated me to declutter my entire home—and I'm not a neat person—but I was motivated by the new energy and freedom that resulted from my efforts.

Types of Clutter-Visible and Mental

Visible clutter robs you of the ability to control your physical environment. It drains your energy and diminishes creativity and productivity. Mental or emotional clutter prevents you from seeing your own natural attractiveness. While time clutter results in busy-ness without productivity, relational clutter results in poor communication and the inability to set appropriate personal boundaries. Health and wellness clutter and financial clutter are often in the forefront as well. Every aspect of your life has the potential to be a haven for clutter.

A common misconception about clutter is that you can organize it. The logical question is "why organize what you don't need?" No matter the form, clutter is an energy drainer—it should be discarded, not organized. The best solution for clutter is to get rid of it. Let's explore specific areas of clutter to more deeply understand how it might look in your environment.

Physical Clutter

A familiar place to start your clutter analysis is by reviewing the physical space in your home and work environments. Everyone can relate to the feeling you get as you enter a room filled with stuff. The room seems to close in on you. Immediately, the question that comes to mind

A common misconception about clutter is that you can organize it.

is "what's going on in here?" You literally sense that there's not enough space in the room for everything that you see.

Whenever I enter a room where piles of clutter are growing, I feel like each pile is calling my name and demanding my attention. My initial thought is to get out of the room and avoid the problem. That works for a little while until I need something that is in one of those piles of clutter.

I wasted more mental energy trying to stay out of the room than I would have used in simply taking the time to declutter the room. The clutter kept me from seeing I had the ability to take care of the matter. The average person spends at least one hour everyday looking for lost or misplaced items. Knowing where everything is gives you an additional 45 eight hour days to invest in something else. In addition to the time savings, you bypass reliving the emotional journey; that's priceless all on its own.

Generally speaking, physical clutter is a symptom of what is going on inside. At the same time, an extreme pre-occupation with cleanliness and order can become an unhealthy obsession and an additional source of stress. There is an amazing amount of relief that occurs as one brings their physical space into order. Clutter is typical of chaos; a lack of clutter moves you closer to peace and tranquility. Many have said to have such peace when they know their affairs are in order. That is the same peace that occurs as you get your physical space in order.

The average person spends at least one hour everyday looking for lost or misplaced items.

Everyone benefits when your time is released to work on more enjoyable activities. In today's culture, there are tremendous pulls on our lives to remain balanced as we juggle many different plates. While not a new struggle, it is certainly one that we are all familiar with. Having your physical environment work with you rather than against you removes one more obstacle from the path of realizing your full potential. There is something about clean and organized surroundings that can help you see tomorrow. You think more clearly when you are in a physical space that is organized, clean and efficient. Clearing your decks of physical clutter provide a great foundation on which to clear clutter in your mental space.

Mental Clutter

An often overlooked, but extremely important area of clutter collection occurs in your mental and emotional space. Just as a home has many storage compartments, so does your mind. During your lifetime, you have had many experiences, learnings and personal encounters stored in your memory banks. Some of those experiences are worth holding on to and others need to be discarded.

The worst place to store clutter is in your mind!

Every home needs spring cleaning to get rid of clutter, and so does your mind. Its storage spaces become filled with past experiences and memories that need to be removed. The worst place to store clutter is in your mind. Overloaded brains act a lot like overloaded computer memory—they crash and stop operating. Since people can't add more memory to their mental capacity, periodically clearing out your mental space can keep you from crashing.

Mental clutter is the accumulation of negative recurring ideas and thoughts. The memory of past experiences can propel us forward with optimism or shackle us with fear. Mental clutter impacts how you see yourself. It hangs around diverting your attention and focus from future success. Negative self talk and judgments are mental clutter that influences what you believe you can achieve. The emotional clutter of past grudges has caused many to remain "stuck" for their entire lifetime.

The saying, "your attitude determines your altitude" is a familiar and very true principle. In other words to increase your altitude, clear your decks of "stinking thinking." Stinking thinking is negative perceptions held by you or others regarding your self image or capabilities. Negative self talk results when we hold on to repeated negative messages about our physical image, capabilities and potential. If a message is repeated often enough, you begin to believe it—even though it is not truth. And since what you do is a product of what you believe, you begin a cycle of self doubt and underachievement. Your mind justifies for you why you cannot move out of your current dilemma. In other words, mental clutter takes away your power of choice. You may even ask yourself why other people seem to believe they can accomplish their goals and you do not have a clue as to what it takes.

If a message is repeated often enough, you begin to believe it—even though it is not truth.

The key to transforming your life begins and ends with "who do I believe I am and what do I think about myself." No matter your life's experience, how and what you think about yourself will determine the measure of success in your life. If you believe you can achieve a particular goal, with the right preparation you will achieve the goal. On the other hand, no amount of preparation can bring success if you believe that you cannot achieve the goal. Without the inner belief that achievement of the goal is a certainty, no amount of preparation can make it happen. It's the age old self-fulfilling prophesy—it is alive and well even today.

If you are steeped in self doubt and reruns of bad life experiences, unrealized potential will be the result. An attitude that is cluttered with self doubt and misconceptions about your potential and abilities will keep you grounded in lesser pursuits. How you think about yourself is a definite indicator of the existence of clutter in your attitude. You are what you believe about yourself.

It is impossible to think negatively about yourself and have a positive outlook. You know what this looks like when you see it —the future never looks bright. Every possibility is met with, "that doesn't work for me" or "it never happen like that for me."

From this perspective, not only is the sky falling, but the entire world seems to be collapsing all the time. Everyone has a bad day, but when a bad day becomes your existence, it is time to clear your mental decks before your ship sinks in despair.

Without clearing the decks, attempts at developing a positive attitude have a negative taint. This is so because you can't see the future vision. Everything looks bleak and unattainable. It is impossible to be what you do not believe that you **Today's mindset is a result of yesterday's experiences.** are. Many find themselves in this contradiction. They desire to be different, but continue to think in a negative fashion about who they are. They fail to realize that how you behave or act is a direct result of what you think about and how you think about yourself.

While it is not the deciding factor, environment and experiences are important factors that shape your attitude about yourself. How we think about ourselves is shaped by our life experiences growing up, going to school, friends we selected and our general environment. Today's mindset is a result of yesterday's experiences. Thankfully, the present allows you the opportunity of choosing to respond and react differently. The landscape of our life's experience can't change, but we can be aware of its impact and not allow clutter to limit who we believe we can become.

For example, let's take a look at environment for a moment. I grew up in a small coal town in West Virginia. From my environment I had a small perspective of a bigger tomorrow. As an avid reader, my perspective was expanded as I attended school. I read books that talked about other places and professions, but it had not become a part of my personal experience. Other professions were theoretical or just something I read—not something I thought I could become.

Now, let's fast forward to graduating from high school and attending Howard University in Washington, DC. As I personally experienced the seeing and being of something bigger than I had seen before, I began to believe I could be something more than what my life's experience had been to date. As I was exposed to other professionals, other lifestyles, ethnic and geographic diversity, my entire perspective of the world changed. I began to "see" what the books I read referred to. I began to experience what the books talked about and I began to think differently about what that meant for me.

Each time I returned home to visit, the environment seemed to get smaller. In reality, it was not getting smaller, but my mindset and experiences were getting larger and expanding to include all of the new things I was seeing and experiencing.

As my desires expanded, I began to yearn for more.

Although armed with expanded experiences, there was still a need to deal with old mindsets and attitudes. Repeated negative messages from my environment that said, "its impossible to make something of yourself." As my desires expanded, I began to yearn for more. I knew there was something pulling me in a different direction. Something was telling me I could rise above my current and past life experiences.

While for many years, I didn't know why I felt that way, I always felt there was more to life than what I was seeing around me. That feeling had much less to do with my environment than it had to do with generally how I was wired on the inside. When the thoughts or opinions are negative, our natural response is to internalize those opinions as true to us in every way. Some of the most difficult clutter clearing has to do with removing from our minds the negative things that have been said about us by people who have been close to us.

It's hard to move past the belief that "you will not amount to much." That one statement can keep you in a holding pattern of doubt and unbelief, though you may have in your hand every tool you need. But having the confidence to use the tools is another thing. As a result, you stay in a holding pattern on life's runway, waiting for someone to say you have been cleared to take off. Many in this position waiting for someone's ok to be more than whom they currently are.

The fact of the matter is you are the one who clears yourself for take off. If you wait for the permission of others, you may spend your life doing just that. Take accountability for developing a personal value statement. You transmit to others what you believe about yourself. **Finish each day and be done with it.** Even when you don't say what is on your mind, your thoughts are revealed through your body language. Actions always speak louder than words. Mental clutter leads to avoidance and procrastination. In summary, Ralph Waldo Emerson gave timely advice that we can use to dispose of mental clutter. "Finish each day and be done with it. You have done what you could. Some blunders and absurdities no doubt crept in; forget them as soon as you can. Tomorrow is a new day; you shall begin it well and serenely. The Holy Bible says it like this "forget those things which are behind, press toward your calling. (Philippians 3:13)

Time Clutter

Time is the great equalizer—everyone gets the same amount each day—24 hours. Since it can't be replaced, time is a more valuable resource than money. Time clutter is spending time on any activity that mean absolutely nothing to you. Clutter free time creates space for engaging in things that matter most to you. This doesn't mean you selfishly spend time alone, it means how you use your time is anchored in your values. Time clutter is busy-ness without productivity. Without a doubt, busy people are usually not effective unless they are spending the majority of their time on high priority matters. Low value activities are not connected to your personal values. Notorious time clutter includes cell phones, email, and an inability to say no. How many hours have you wasted by agreeing to complete a project that had absolutely no value to you?

Health and Financial Clutter

This form of clutter occurs when you neglect your physical and financial health. In some cases, they are directly related. Problems in the health area usually lead to

Time clutter is busy-ness without productivity

problems in your finances. The converse is true as well—both lead to increased physical and mental stress. Each one can have catastrophic impact if not dealt with in a timely and consistent manner.

As a bankruptcy attorney, I have witnessed first hand the mental and emotional stress for individuals and businesses that find themselves in the unfortunate position of considering this legal option. In extreme financial stress, decisions that seem so obviously wrong to most, suddenly become attractive options. They become attractive because your view is obscured by emotional clutter resulting from the financial need. When bankruptcy is the only alternative, my role includes preparing clients for the feelings they will experience and to equip them to rebuild their credit and develop habits to keep short accounts with financial clutter. I'm sure the medical profession has witnessed similar results with health clutter. Time, health and financial clutter have a tremendous impact on your mental well being.

Clutter's Consequences

Proverbs 23:7 says it this way, "As a man thinketh in his heart, so he is." Without a doubt, what you think, defines who you are and what you can achieve. If you believe success is not available to you, it won't be. If you believe you can jump to the moon, everything in you cooperates to make jumping to the moon a possibility. The very nature of clutter is to hold you back—it's holding on to stuff you don't need. A cluttered lifestyle is full of missed opportunities and unending procrastination. Everything takes twice the effort.

Decluttering is essential to allowing your natural attractiveness to rise to the surface. Making room for you is the desired outcome of clearing your space. There's something about clear space that permits the mind and its creativity to expand beyond its usual boundaries. My experience has been that life has a lot more potential when you can see clearly ahead of you and you have made space for what you value most.

Clutter accumulates from the ordinary events of our lives. We go from one activity to the next—rarely taking time to reflect on lessons learned. Our society promotes living in the moment—no time for reflection or future planning. You rarely see the need to clear the decks when you live in the moment. Not clearing the decks means that you live your life with many impediments that are

> **"As a man thinketh in his heart, so he is."**
> Proverbs 23:7

capable of being moved out of the way. You spend unnecessary energy working around clutter. You constantly second guess or regret your decisions and lose valuable time. As I look back at some of my biggest blunders, I realize they were the result of cluttered decks that obscured my point of view. Not all of the choices were bad choices—they just weren't the best choices. A clearer deck would have led me to different decisions.

Sometimes you need motivation to clear your decks. My motivation was a feeling of being underutilized in my former corporate role. This was my conclusion after I cleared my mental space to get a clear picture of what was causing my dissatisfaction. Once the decks were clear, I could plan a strategy to address the dissatisfaction. Prior to clearing decks, leaving the organization was not a desired alternative. At the end of my journey, I realized that no matter the roles or the organizations, my everyday work needed to leverage my strengths and preferences to keep me engaged. At that moment in time, I realized I no longer fit the role the organization was willing to pay me to do. Clearing out mental clutter empowered me to arrive at this conclusion and take the next step of pursuing a role that would allow me to use my gifts and talents.

Once I cleared my decks, I could see my future potential and with confidence, I knew the next step was up to me. If my life was going to be different, I had to take action to make it different. Without clear decks, this decision would have never risen to the surface to be answered. In most cases, it is a negative circumstance or extraordinary life event that becomes the motivation for change. You are individually accountable for shaping your destiny. Active participation is a requirement for reaching your full potential. Passive reaction to life creates a mindset that lacks vision and satisfaction. It is like taking a trip, but never really expecting to arrive at the destination.

Getting rid of clutter

Seemingly overwhelming, significant progress can be made by adhering to the mindset of taking small steps toward the end result. Every major accomplishment begins with a small step.

Clearing out the clutter is the process by which we create an environment that encourages and nurtures who we are. Clearing out the clutter releases creativity and creates vision and provides the opportunity to address old issues as you journey to a new and better place.

This is also one of those processes you do not truly appreciate until it is over. Approach it with the mindset of the practical purposes the clutter serves. If it enhances, equips and keeps you focused on the future—*keep it.* Clearing clutter causes you to take a look at messy collections that may have been around for a long **Clearing out the clutter releases creativity and creates vision...** time. Some of your collections may have even been covered up in the hope that they would disappear on their own.

Clearing your personal space puts you in the position of making choices that are aligned with your personal values. Once the clutter is cleared, it is like an "aha moment." You see the same circumstances with the same eyes, but you see with a different attitude, a different perspective. That's the benefit of clearing out the clutter. It's not that you get a new you, but you gain a new mindset and a new perspective. As has been said by many before, success is 90% attitude and 10% ability.

Much of corporate professional development with employees is spent on reshaping employees to get rid of their stinking thinking that hinders business objectives. Every organization is the sum total of the individuals that make up the organization. Even though it sounds good, it does not have lasting effects because workplace development deals with what you do, not who you are. How you react in the workplace culture is a result of who you are and for the best results companies should deal with who their employees are as well as what they do. Without a doubt, unless change is anchored in individual core values, it cannot be sustained over time and will result in additional training expenses.

This is not an indictment against workplace training. It is a wake up call to the workplace employee to get a whole life. It is each individual's accountability to be responsible for becoming naturally attractive and maximizing their potential. Waiting on the workplace to do this for you is an ill-conceived plan. Think about it, the latest job movement statistics indicate that most people will work for a new employer ever three to five years. And as we all know, every employer wants you to understand their environment and how they think in their culture. In your work career, assume that our work life spans from 20 to 70 years of age, with an average tenure of five years, you have the potential to change employers at least ten times. If only half of those changes occur, without knowing who we are, we will be schizophrenic by the time we enter retirement because ever employer attempts to rebuild us to their standard.

It's a wake up call to the workplace employee to get a whole life.

This book is about cutting out the reinvention and giving your family, workplace and community the best of who you are based on your work of self discovery. Take inventory of the clutter that's around you. Pay attention and identify the negative repetitive messages lurking about your perspective of you. Get rid of stinking thinking once and for all. For some, this may be a simple as acknowledging their existence. For others, your thinking may need the assistance of trained coaches or therapists. Whatever your situation, just do it. Start today to peel back the layers of the onion to who you really are. Do not allow your own thoughts or the thoughts of others to undermine who you are.

Maintaining Clear Decks

Now that you have successfully cleared the decks, we need to put strategies in place for maintaining your clear space. There are many books on organizing and clearing out clutter. Appendix A contains a listing of decluttering resources. If you need support or work better with a partner, find a clutter buddy to work with. A clutter buddy is someone who shares your same passion for clearing the space. This person can act as an accountability partner to support you along the journey. If you need more structured help, a clutter or personal coach may be the solution. In some cases, it may be more effective for you if you hire an organizer to partner with you as you complete the physical organization of your work and life space.

The more involvement you have in the decluttering process the more you increase your ability to maintain a clutter free environment. If the opportunity is available, work with your organizer to develop the initial space clearing and the maintenance plan. You will immediately see the difference clear space has on your attitude.

You are beginning to see you

At this point in our journey, you should begin to see a clearer picture of you and what you desire for your life. Clear decks provide the best vantage point to begin your journey. The length of the process depends on the amount and intensity of the clutter that is around you. Don't focus on the time it will take to clear the space, focus on the benefits of an uncluttered life. Every small step is important. Start out slow and allow the decluttering process to fully run its course.

Short changing the process can prevent discovering root causes of the source of clutter. There was a beginning to everything. Knowing the root cause helps to effectively eliminate clutter permanently. In her book, *Clear Your Clutter with Feng*

Shui, organizing guru, Karen Kingston, states that accumulating clutter has three primary motivators—you are wired to do it; you resist letting go of anything and society encourages you to gather as much stuff as you can.

Clear the decks of all clutter —remember clutter has only one purpose—to hold you back. Finish the process of moving through all of the areas, even though there may be continuing work to do in each area. You're not looking for a quick fix. You are about to undertake the most important step of your life.Clear decks and a decluttered life-style permit your natural attractiveness to rise to the surface and allow the transformation process to begin.

remember clutter has only one purpose — to hold you back

When you move ahead without addressing all of the areas, you actually create more work for yourself and false starts. Once you experience a clutter free life, you are more effective, productive and spontaneous. Instead of avoiding the clutter, you actually start to look for it because removing it brings greater peace of mind. The first time I completed a clutter project, I wanted to spend all of my time in that room. The sense of order and peace was phenomenal—so much so that organizing all the other rooms was a task I looked forward to with anticipation and excitement.

Once you have completed the process, you now have a simple template you can use to maintain clear space and to bring order out of chaos. Maintaining clear decks should be a routine part of goal setting for every month. Take inventory each month; learn to keep a short account with clutter. As the poet Alexander Pope said, "Order is heaven's first law." Keeping a short account is a key strategy to preventing the "sneak up" effect. Now that you can see you, let's begin our journey to understanding the real you and what motivates and inspires you.

Key Learnings

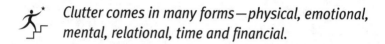 Clutter comes in many forms—physical, emotional, mental, relational, time and financial.

Ӿ No matter the form, clutter drains energy, vision, productivity and potential.

Ӿ Clutter obscures your natural attractiveness.

Ӿ Clutter should be released—not organized—get rid of it.

Ӿ Maintaining a clutter free environment is an ongoing and continuous process.

Chapter Two
Discovering My Values

"He who understands others is learned,
he who understands himself is wise."
—Lao Tse

Introduction

Wisdom calls us to have the deepest understanding of one thing, ourselves. Your ability to achieve full potential increases exponentially when you are armed with a clear understanding of yourself. Not knowing yourself almost certainly ensures that your life's journey will include many dead ends. Opportunities pursued, but not completed; dreams attempted, but that somehow died, seemingly without good reason. Identifying values is the first place to start when you are experiencing a lack of meaning and fulfillment in any area of your life. When our values are being satisfied, life seems wonderful. When those same values go unfulfilled, our present seems full of confusion and conflict and the future doesn't seem to exist.

After completing the decluttering process, you should begin to see the silhouette of the real you beginning to emerge. This shadow of who you are is free from the limiting opinions of others, baggage of previous experiences and your own self-limiting perceptions. Suspend your critical analysis and judgmental attitude to allow yourself the space to connect with who you are and what brings meaning to your life. Life's natural pace has a way of pulling us away from what is important to us. We often forget to keep our values as the first priority. And if the truth be told, we even forget what we value or fail to acknowledge that we never knew what it was to begin with.

Core values impact every decision we make. Though unaware of the specific value in play, we all have guiding principles that govern the choices we make. Now more than ever, the ability to make effective life and career choices is paramount to achieving potential. The more your values find the opportunity to be satisfied, the more rewarding and meaningful is your life experience. Aware- ness and understanding of those values benefit us by providing the hidden meaning in our lives. You can easily recall times when you were passionate about a particular subject, but didn't understand the basis for the passion. In all likelihood, one of your core values was in play or being infringed upon and it got your attention.

> Nothing is so powerful as an insight into human
> nature... what compulsions drive a man, what
> instincts dominate his action. If you know these
> things about a person, you can touch him at the
> core of his being.
>
> —*William Bernbach*

The conscious identification of core values has somehow slipped past most of us. It is more of an exceptional circumstance that an individual is fully aware of and can clearly define their values. Values are not hard to find, but for some reason we don't tend to look for them until some major life catastrophe occurs. Rather than allowing catastrophe to be the catalyst, this chapter is designed to put you in the driver's seat of discovering your values. We will define values, the benefits of knowing your values, how you obtain your values and how to identify and understand your values. As the captain of your ship, your ability to pursue a life of meaning and significance is a matter of choice. You decide which imprint to leave with your family, community and in the world.

Clarifying your values and integrating them as a lifestyle is easier said than done. Our task in this chapter is to bring the picture of who you are into focus, with more clarity and definition. By uncovering the unique threads that run through everything you do, you will see a clearer picture of who you are and will be able to identify those things that touch you at the core of your being.

What are values?

Simply speaking, values are your personal assessment of what you consider most important in life. They help us to determine what's worthwhile and in some cases, what's right or wrong, good or bad. Values are the principles which guide your choices— they are what you are fundamentally committed to above all other things. Values provide direction, point toward purpose, motivate us and provide a sense of fulfillment and a roadmap for decision making. Our values are immutable characteristics of who we are. You have more than one value and some values have a higher priority than others. None are absolute, but take their appropriate place in the values hierarchy depending on your current life needs.

In research by Shalom Schwartz, a professor at Hebrew University, studies suggest that values are guiding principles that influence your decisions and actions. Values are persuasive and enduring and permeate every aspect of our lives. The idea that there is a hierarchy of values that are based on individual and universal human needs is not a new idea. We see similar findings in the work of Maslow who believed that human beings are motivated by our unsatisfied needs—meaning we will seek to satisfy unmet needs first and in a specific order.

We all have physical and biological survival needs. Lower needs must be fulfilled before a person will seek to fulfill higher needs that relate to self actualization, social interaction or community welfare.

SELF ACTUALIZATION

ESTEEM

LOVE

SAFETY

PHYSIOLOGICAL

Why are values important?
Understanding your personal values is important to developing confidence for life's journey and to maintaining a stick-to-it-ness to make it through to the end. Your values are the hidden motivators and untapped energy sources that will get you where you want to go. Your values are an encouraging internal source that will propel you forward when external circumstances say "give up—it's not worth it." If you understand your values, you understand your core motivations. Without this understanding, you unconsciously choose to aimlessly float through life wondering why and how you continue to make the same wrong choices. It's that nagging question of "how did I get here again? I thought I had this all figured out."

Values are to be distinguished from passions. Passions are emotions. At times, passions are unbridled and uncontrolled. When your values are in play, they are usually accompanied by a passionate feeling. You should be passionate about your values, but do not let passion be the sole determinant of your values. When passions drive your values, you find your-

Your values are the hidden motivators and untapped energy sources that will get you where you want to go.

self with a new set of values every week. True passions are emotions distinguished from reason. Passions are intense, driving and they can be overwhelming. In the moment, they cause you to feel like you are on the right track, but under calmer circumstances, we often wish we had taken a different route.

On the other hand, being passionate about your values can be the difference between enjoying your life's journey and seeing it as an adventure and a viewpoint that your life is absolutely boring without a hint of excitement. When you are passionate

Everyone needs a systematic approach to sort through the avalanche of choices.

about your values, every decision and every action flows through your value filter. Your very attitude and mindset are affected by your values. Your values determine who you are and how you choose to arrive at your destination. The priority you place on specific values can change at different stages of your life.

In short, bringing focus to our values means understanding what it is that makes us tick. It answers the question of when you are most fulfilled, what it is you are doing and which value is in motion at that time. Peter Drucker, founding father of the study of management states that self management is the biggest challenge for the 21st century person. We are overwhelmed with choices—bad, good and perfect choices. Everyone needs a systematic approach to sort through the avalanche of choices. Identifying your values and using those values as you make decisions will lead to choices that take you closer to fulfilling your life purpose. Values based decision making requires reflection time—time to slow down and reflect on what's important. Taking that time to slow down and reflect accelerates decision making down the road.

Reflection time has almost been cut out of our lifestyle. Without reflection time, life is in a state of a perpetual limbo— with too many open switches that need closing. When in limbo, Career Coach, Richard Leider, advises "you have to unpack your bag and then repack it, so you can go on to the next phase of your life." Take the time now to unpack your values bag and repack according to what's important to you. Don't fall into the trap of believing you will get a different result if you continue the same behavior— everyone knows that's insanity. Identify your values, integrate them into your lifestyle and be a witness to the transformation that occurs.

Where do values come from?

Values originate from three primary sources—your childhood environment, culture and work environment. Values can be consciously or unconsciously chosen, or arrived at by default. Your family of origin provided you with your first model of values in action. Sometimes you become what you see, even without affirmatively choosing to do so. At other times, your conscious rejection of a particular value is your conscious choice to adopt an opposing value.

Our society and culture create values that are important to its survival. American popular culture places value on consumerism— the accumulation of material wealth and doing, constantly looking for the next achievement. When our main values focus is externally driven, it's easy to overlook the importance of taking the time to invest in the value of "being who we are." Yet this internally focused value holds the most promise of moving you toward reaching your full potential and pursing your life purpose.

Society's definition of self worth is to look at what you have and what you do. "Being who you are" is little more than a notion and certainly not a pursuit that is encouraged. Society doesn't define success as getting what you want and enjoying the journey—but, that's exactly what success is. In his book, *The Strangest Secret*, Earl Nightingale defines success as the progressive realization of a worthy idea. In other words, if you deliberately intended to end up at specific destination, you're good at what you do and you enjoy the journey, success is written all over your life whether society acknowledges it or not.

Constant focus on acquiring things and nonstop doing results in your self worth being based on material goods and accomplishments. With this formula for underachievement all around us, there is no wondering as to why so many people feel like their lives are without purpose and meaning. In the book *Human Being* by Dave Ellis and Stan Lankowitz, the ultimate formula for complete fulfillment is integrating all three areas—being, doing and having—with the main emphasis on "being who you are." Neither what you have nor what you do can replace the satisfaction that comes from having the freedom to be who you are and live your life according to your values.

While some values are determined overtime, others come more quickly. For example, if you have recently experienced a health crisis—heart attack, breast cancer diagnosis or other significant medical condition—you might instantly choose to value a healthier lifestyle and immediately change your behavior to reflect your new value. Let's turn our attention to the conscious pursuit of discovering your values.

Step One—*Discovering Your Values*

There are many ways to discover your values. How you discover them is not as important as making the actual discovery. Behavior experts offer many different approaches to discovering values. In this section, we'll review several different approaches that have worked effectively for many persons. Choose the approach that best suits your style and get started on your journey. At the end of your journey, don't be surprised if your values seem to match some very familiar institutions in society or even values your parents held.

The most important step of the discovery process is acknowledging and accepting your values—in other words, owning the values because they speak to the essence of your life. Armed with your values, they become a clear guide to who you are and what you can become.

In *Values, A Key To Meaningful Work,* Mark Guterman and Terry Karp discuss several methods to discovering your values. This next section is a compilation of their methods and other resources designed to help you identify your core essence.

Journaling

Journaling is one of the simplest ways to come in contact with your values. It connects you with your inner self and provides the opportunity to document your experiences and the corresponding emotions associated with the experiences. Journaling is an excellent time to acknowledge and reflect on your true feelings. As you reflect and conduct this inner dialogue, you are likely to uncover the specific value that's being utilized.

As an exercise, journaling can take as little or as much time as your schedule permits. You can start with 15 minutes per day and build up to the time frame that works for you. Some persons have more than one journal to cover different subjects. Writing down your feelings and emotions helps you address your mental chatter by identifying your values and when they are being nurtured or when they are in conflict.

> Journaling is an excellent time to acknowledge and reflect on your true feelings.

When journaling to determine values, ask yourself what is important to you and whether you feel good about this value being important to you. Because journaling is reflection, it is only as effective as your honesty with yourself. It brings you face to face with your life issues. Confronting your inner conflicts requires honesty with yourself and truth about the impact this value has in your life. At this point, you have a decision to make—will you move forward to resolve the issue or will you just let sleeping dogs lie?

Journaling during transition is a great way to sort out the pros and cons of different scenarios. My journaling allows me to critically analyze my emotions. It's like taking a snapshot in time and understanding your underlying motivation for decisions. By writing things down, I was able to identify objective demonstrations of specific values in operation.

I used journaling to sort out the benefits and review those benefits in light of my values as I considered whether to leave the comfort and security of a corporate environment for entrepreneurial pursuits. When I finalized my decision to leave, I knew without a doubt that the decision was right for me and my family. Values based decisions take away the second thoughts and regretful decisions. I was able to move forward without looking back and wondering if I had made the right decision.

Lifeline Exercises

For those who would like to understand how they develop their current values, lifeline exercises provide the opportunity to highlight key decision points throughout your lifetime. Some like to look at the exercise as reviewing your defining moments—circumstances that caused you to make a significant life change. You acquire values from your life experiences. These experiences include your family relations, society, others in your environment and yourself. Everyone has defining moments where we know that our lives are what they are today because of the choices we made at that time. A defining moment for me was my decision to go to an out of state school for my college education. My value of autonomy and independence motivated the decision to go to a place where I had never been and had no visible support system. This was a value I saw in my parents. Since all of their relatives seemed to live in other states, it seemed natural to me to venture off to a new location. Some 20 years later, I still experience the benefits of that decision and still find that value actively in play.

Genograms

If you have a huge appreciation for family, your values discovery may be enhanced by using a genogram. A genogram is a brief history drawn to resemble a family tree. The genogram extends beyond the immediate family to include other significant relationships. As you take a look at these relationships, make note of your relationship with the person, their work, and the messages you received from that person about work and the values that were transferred to you. For example, in my genogram, I have a reference to my 10th grade teacher, Dorothy Smith.

Ms. Smith taught World Civilizations and took great care to help us understand the subject matter and our specific place in world history. She imparted to me the values of being involved in our nation's civic process and being proud of the opportunity to participate. She gave her class a thorough knowledge of the entire process and as a result, I retained the value of pursing knowledge with a purpose in mind—to do my part. I was sold on voting, jury duty and voicing an opinion for my chosen candidates and any other topic for that matter.

Values Inventories

There are several value inventories or value clarification exercises freely available on education and coaching websites. They range from the basic listing of values to consider to those that include self directed homework assignments. Since we spend 60% of our time at work, some of the tools divide values into two categories—work and personal or include an additional category for family values. Remember, values are personal and unique. Use the categories that work for you—the categories are not as important as the discovery. Any listing is designed to jumpstart your discovery process of what's important to you. Here is a sample listing of work and personal values that you might see listed. Knowing that it's not possible to include everyone's values, most inventories ask that you add any values that are important to you that may not be contained on their list.

Values Inventories

Sample Values Listing

Achievement	Helping Others	Ability to Influence	Friendships	Making Decisions
Excitement	Education	Peace of Mind	Pioneering	Power
Love	Justice	Loyalty	Health	Happiness
Reputation	Truth	Wealth	Music	Neatness
Challenge	Material Possessions	Ethics	Flexibility	Honesty
Leisure time	Creativity	Personal Appearance	Power	Sense of Control
Spiritual development	Intellectual Stimulation	Loyalty	Teamwork	Leading others
Working Alone	Helping Society	Aesthetics	Independence	Security
Fast Pace	Supporting Family	Quality Time	Financial Freedom	Physical Challenge
Adventure	Precision and Accuracy	Diversity	Knowledge	Integrity

As you review the list of values, select values that resonate with what's important to you. Everyone can identify with most of the values and you may need a method to determine the priority of your values. Once you've made your list, assign a ranking to each value using the following scale and begin with the values that are very important to you all the time.

1–Not important at all
2–Important sometimes
3–Important all the time

You may identify with a value, but that value is not important to you all the time. For example, leisure time is important to me sometimes, but my spiritual development is important to me all of the time. My value of spiritual development is more important to me than leisure time. So much so that my leisure time may be spent in spiritual development activities.

Step Two – *Write a personal definition*
The next step is to write a personal definition of each value. Your values should be based on your personal experiences. It is critical that you identify with the value in a way that is important to you. Just choosing a word off of a list doesn't add the clarity needed to provide guidance in a meaningful way. It's important that you understand what's important to you about the particular value.

Step Three – *Own the value*
After understanding the value's importance to you, there's a need to "own that value." Ask yourself, "is this really me?" If not, take the liberty to set that value aside for another one. Another aspect of ownership is your ability to freely choose the value. Values originate from many sources—some are original with you, others are gathered from the wisdom around you. Whatever the source, the values you repack should be your own and should be an inner reflection of who you are. Take an affirmative role in choosing your values. Don't be concerned if your chosen values seem familiar. The more important aspect is that you made the choice to adopt the value. Outward evidence of an inward passion is evident when you talk to a person about something or someone they value. Their energy is contagious and it can't be contained—it's seeing "passion in action." Values are fluid and change over time depending where we are in the stage of life. Whatever the case and whether it involves career, family or community involvement, understanding your values empower you to integrate them into every area of your life.

Once these steps have been taken, you should be well on your way to developing your values. Some professionals advocate taking additional steps beyond the values inventory to see if patterns or themes develop. In New Directions in Career Planning and the

Workforce, Mark Guterman and Terry Karp created *ValueSearch* based on Schwartz's work, they suggest grouping your values after they are identified to gain an even deeper understanding of the real you and to bring more clarity to potential conflicts. They believe that most values fall into the following categories that they define as follows:

U-Universality: Understanding, appreciation, tolerance and protection of the welfare of all people and of nature.

B-Benevolence: Concern for the protection and enhancement of the welfare of people with whom one is in frequent contact.

T-Tradition: Respect for, commitment to, and acceptance of customs and ideas that one's culture or religion expects of individuals.

S-Security: Desire for safety, harmony, and stability of society, relationships, and self.

P-Power: Attainment of social status, prestige, influence, authority, or leadership of people and resources.

A-Achievement: Desire for personal success or accomplishment. Need to demonstrate competence in everyday life.

E-Excitement: Seek pleasure or sensuous gratification. Enjoy unpredictability and variety in life.

SD-Self Direction: Pursue independent thought or action. Enjoy the ability to choose, create, and explore.

Bill Bonnstetter, founder and President of Target Training International, states in his book, *"If I Knew Then What I Know Now"* these six attitudes that are the "why" of what moves us to action. He believes that your top two attitudes motivate your decisions and action.

Theoretical Attitude: A passion to know, seek out, understand and systematize the truth.

Utilitarian Attitude: A passion to gain a return on all investments involving time, money and resources.

Aesthetic Attitude: A passion to enjoy and experience my impressions of the world around me and allow them to mold me into all I can be.

Individualistic Attitude: A drive to control your own destiny, a passion to lead.

Social Attitude: A passion to invest myself, my time and my resources into helping others achieve their potential.

Traditional Attitude: A passion to find and pursue the highest meaning in life, in the divine and in the ideal.

In both instruments, every individual has two priority values that motivate them to take action. The more in sync your environments are with your top two values, the more meaning and value will exist in your work, social and family environments. The end result is the opportunity to express these motivations which lead to more individual satisfaction.

Step Four–*Putting my values into action*

The key point of discovering your values is to be able to integrate those values in decision making. Application of the values to your decisions adds meaning to your decisions and moves you closer to reaching your full potential. When your actions are in sync with your values, there is a sense of "everything is going well." When your actions are not in sync, you feel unbalanced and like things are not working. Everyone desires to contribute to the value of life. Surveys of older adults indicate that one of the four things they would do over if they had the opportunity is to understand at an earlier time what brought fulfillment and satisfaction to their lives. Putting values into action enables the contribution to occur. Other universal desires include the need to have a deep connection with the creative spirit of life and to know and express your gifts and talents.

> Putting values into action enables the contribution to occur.

I can point to changes in my career when I could identify that certain aspects of my work or relationships touched upon my values. Those changes led to feelings of loss when certain activities took on lesser importance in my day to day activities. For example, when I transitioned from the private practice of law to head up an administrative agency, I greatly missed the one–on-one contact and individual relationship building that was a large part of my private practice. It was after the transition that I became aware of this value for interpersonal relationships. At the time, there was a logical reason for the transition—I wanted the opportunity to gain leadership experience. Eventually, as I became more aware of this and other values, my career choices led me back to one-on-one relationships.

Look back over your career or family decisions and identify changes in your work or family life that caused you to say to yourself, "I really miss doing those things." In some cases, knowing what you don't like can help identify a personal value. I recall taking a legal role where my primary motivator was the high salary. The role did not provide the opportunity for me to use my strengths or have the opportunity for one-on-one contact.

While money was the initial attraction, the attraction quickly faded and I became acutely aware that it takes more than money for me to experience career fulfillment. Since that time, money has been one of many considerations and has a lower priority in terms of "must haves" for the role. Don't get me wrong, competitive pay a consideration, it just doesn't make or break the decision for me any longer. My personal and coaching experiences reaffirm that money is not everything. Enjoying what you do, being good at it and getting paid is a much better formula than just getting paid.

While my career choices had been varied, each choice allowed me to have direct impact on the lives of people I came into contact with. I was able to move away from this work for a specific season and purpose. I always knew I would eventually seek out one on one contact as an integral part of the work I do everyday. Understanding your values ensures you will make better decisions during times of transition. My decisions on the new role would have centered on the question of "are my values engaged as a part of my daily activities?" Just as these experiences became career value markers for me, you will be able to identify markers in your life that will help you get an idea of your values. You will also be able to identify what you naturally enjoy about your work.

Resolving conflicts in values

Values conflicts occur when meeting the needs of two values would require opposite action. Values conflicts can be internal or external. They are internal when they occur as you pursue individual values. They are external when they involve the values of others. One way to resolve the conflict is to have a values hierarchy. In simple conflicts, it can be done in advance— for more complex conflicts, you may want to consider any changes that have occurred since you last reviewed your values. Keep in mind that your hierarchy is not absolute; it's ok to adjust the priority—not the values themselves —based on current reality.

> The most effective way to deal with values conflicts is to acknowledge them and gain a better understanding of the "why" of the conflict.

The most effective way to deal with values conflicts is to acknowledge them and gain a better understanding of the "why" of the conflict. Understanding the "why" often leads to resolution of the conflict. If you're unable to resolve the conflict on your own, coaches and a trusted accountability partner are great sounding boards to help you sort out the conflicts. Ignoring values conflicts stops your forward progress until the conflict is resolved. Unless you deal with them, unresolved values conflicts can hang around through out your lifetime. Their manifestations include under-achievement, unused potential, unused gifts, talents and strengths.

Summary

Values are an integral part of our lives—whether we consciously choose them or not. Your personal values should be the foundation upon which everything else in your life is built. Take for instance the Chinese Bamboo Tree. In its first four years of growth, the growth takes place underground. It is invisible to the eye except for a tiny shoot. Unseen to the eye is the extraordinary growth that is occurring underground, which will enable the tree to have phenomenal growth in its fifth year. In the fifth year the tree can grow up to 80 feet.

Taking the time to slow down and pattern your life according to your values can lead to a "fifth year" of phenomenal personal growth. Your fifth year can occur in one month, three months, one year or more. Your determination is key to shortening the time between being a tiny sprout and growing 80 feet. How important is it to you to live a life that is authentic and naturally attractive? If this is an important value for you, these next chapters will lead to a transformed life.

Values are an integral part of our lives— whether we consciously choose them or not.

Key Learnings

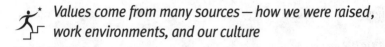

Values come from many sources — how we were raised, work environments, and our culture

Take the time to identify, define, own and implement your values into your lifestyle

Consciously chosen values propel you forward in reaching your potential

Seek out and resolve all values conflicts

Chapter Three
Strengths, Talents, Skills and Abilities

"You can do anything, but not everything."
—*Anonymous*

Introduction

Using your strengths to achieve results positively impacts every area of your life. In the world of work, Peter Drucker states that "most American workers have no idea what their strengths are …when asked, most people will give you a blank stare or the wrong answer." Either answer is unacceptable since natural talents are easily discovered and developed into strengths.

The first time I was asked about my strengths, I responded with the typical blank stare. I was pretty certain I had some talent, but I couldn't identify them for me or anyone else. Like most people, I began with a discussion of what I enjoyed doing—a definite characteristic—but not the total picture. Even if I could have identified them, I certainly had no idea how to use this knowledge to help me make better choices. In hindsight, a couple of my answers were in the right ball park and some were just completely wrong. As a result, my strengths remained in my toolbox as untapped resources.

> Not identifying your strengths is like being the sole heir to a billion dollar estate, but not knowing who you are.

No matter your role—business owner, home caregiver or

employee—it is vital to identify your strengths and find ways to put your strengths in play everyday. Think of your talents like the earth's natural resources; they exist for you to make use of them. They are exactly what you need to achieve your greatest potential. On the other hand, unless they are drawn out and developed, talents are of no benefit. Not identifying your strengths is like being the sole heir to a billion dollar estate, but not knowing who you are. While you are legally entitled to the estate and its benefits, without knowledge of your identity or strengths—you are in the same position as the person with no inheritance. Just like values, lacking knowledge of your strengths is a significant hindrance to developing a meaningful lifestyle and career. I'm not saying you won't have a life, you will, but it will lack important dimensions that bring complete fulfillment and satisfaction.

Every person has the potential for greatness beyond their current abilities.

Here's the answer to why work always seems like hard labor. You're probably in a role where your talents are not engaged in your day to day activities. If you're in the wrong role and you believe what most American workers believe—work should be hard and not enjoyable—you fit the description for a disengaged employee. In the back of your mind, you question whether achieving excellence and greatness is even a possibility for you. You tell yourself you're just an average bear who's not supposed to do great things.

Let me clarify what I mean when I say "do great things." I'm not speaking of greatness for personal accolades. I'm speaking of greatness that brings meaning to the lives of others. It's about seizing the opportunities that come your way to transform a good thing into a great thing. Here's an example. George Clooney, an actor, is known for his talent of bringing others together for a common cause. He seized the opportunity to use that strength to have others to make significant contributions to the Tsunami survivors. He was able to take a good thing—his desire to contribute—and make it a great thing—get his friends to contribute along with him. You don't have to be a Hollywood star to move from good to great. It's available to you right where you are if you know your strengths and are willing to use them as life provides the opportunity.

Every person has the potential for greatness beyond their current abilities. Your strengths are an undeniable facet of who you are and they are your most powerful natural resource. Combined with your personal values, your talents are a powerful force in your toolbox to propel you to achieve great things. If they remain undiscovered it is impossible to reach your full potential or fulfill your life's purpose.

Talents like to masquerade as normal behavior. Activating them is effortless; they know when to kick in. Because they are so automatic, it is hard to distinguish them from everyday behavior. Matter of fact, when you see strengths in action, they seem so normal you may have the mistaken impression that "everyone can do this." Most of the time, we may not be consciously aware that we are using talents or strengths. When others see your strengths in action and compliment, you may recall saying things like "that was nothing, it's not anything special" or with a little effort anybody can do this." But the fact of the matter is that not anybody can—only you can do it in a way that it was just done. Your strengths and talents are specific to you.

Two people can have the same strengths, but in action, those strengths will look different because of our individual uniqueness. Strengths are "natural attractiveness" in action. When you see "strengths in action" you say things like "that looked so easy" or "I can do that." In some cases, maybe you can if you have similar strengths, but it's more likely that your perception of the degree of difficulty has been obscured by seeing natural talent in action. That same mindset causes you to minimize your personal strengths.

While values are capable of changing over time, strengths and talents are hardwired into the core of who you are. They are enduring and immutable; lasting throughout your lifetime and capable of greater development, but not changing. Values or skills can be dropped or added; you are born with your strengths. Over the course of your lifetime, they remain the same. Your talents are one of your greatest resources for reaching your full potential. Don't miss the opportunity to tap into your internal natural resources. You can never deplete your strengths and they are always available to you and capable of being continuously developed.

In this chapter we'll define strengths and explain how they differ from skills, knowledge and abilities. Next, we'll discuss the benefits of knowing your strengths and the different inventories available to facilitate their discovery.

> ...values are capable of changing over time, strengths and talents are hardwired into the core of who you are.

Finally, since a realistic picture of "who you are" includes a look at strengths and weaknesses, we'll spend some time talking about strategies to minimize weaknesses and in what instances is there a need to overcome your strengths.

The desired outcome for this chapter is to put you in a position to know your strengths, develop them and create more opportunities to use them daily. Before you move to the next section, stop and make a list of your strengths. Hold on to the list for use in the next section.

What are strengths and talents?

Macmillan's Dictionary defines strengths as "a strong attribute or inherent asset." Webster's defines talents as the "natural endowment or ability of a superior quality." In many cases, you'll see the words strengths and talents used interchangeably. As defined, both are internal and are an attribute of your natural attractiveness. They are innate qualities of excellence. In "*Now Discover Your Strengths,*" they are described as the ability to provide consistent, near-perfect performance in a given activity and are a combination of skills, talents and knowledge.

> "Ability becomes strength only if you can fathom yourself doing it repeatedly, happily, and successfully."
>
> (*Buckingham-Now Discover Your Strengths*)

This means each time your developed strength is in play, the execution of the strength is successful, near perfect and you can't wait to have the opportunity to use the strength again.

Using this definition, review the list of strengths you made earlier and highlight the strengths that match this definition. Don't worry if your initial list is significantly narrowed or totally depleted. This definition will help you get rid of the mental clutter that has limited your ability to see this aspect of your natural attractiveness. Keep in mind Buckingham's definition refers to fully developed strengths. At this point of the journey, you may not recognize your undeveloped strengths. Like diamonds in the rough, it takes a little polish to bring out a strength's true brilliance. Let's focus on uncovering your raw talent and then we will discuss how to develop the use of that talent to near perfect performance.

What are knowledge, skills and abilities?

Knowledge, skills and abilities are acquired over time through experience, education and training. Unlike natural talents, these are external determinants. Strengths are innate and your unique talent package is established from the time you are born. As you grow up, you acquire education and experience that enables you to develop skills in one or many areas. We gain knowledge from reading, the educational process and from life experiences. Knowledge is the body of factual or experiential information. Skills are the observable demonstration of an activity. Skills and abilities are the most common "wrong answer" that people respond with when asked to describe their strengths. "I'm good with people. I like to help others or I'm a good communicator." All of these are skills or abilities that you develop with experience and as you can see, but unlike strengths, they are not unique to any individual.

Developing a strength is impossible without the building blocks of knowledge, skills and abilities.

Developing a strength is impossible without the building blocks of knowledge, skills and abilities. We learn new skills even though our talents are not in play and they can be acquired in many areas. You are "able" to do a particular skill when you can demonstrate the application of certain knowledge to perform basic steps of an activity. For example, as a college graduate, you gain knowledge in a specific degree area. Experience is added to your knowledge as you learn to perform activities in a given area.

You are "skilled" as you become proficient in performing the activities. Individuals that have more knowledge, skills, abilities and experience than anyone else in a specific area are called experts. Experts who are also using their strengths become giants or extraordinary players in their fields. Review the strengths list that you made at the beginning of the chapter to see how many of the strengths you listed disguised themselves as skills or expertise.

Strengths supersede learning and as Emeril would say, "take it up a couple of notches" the application of knowledge, skills and abilities. Every profession has individuals that rise to the top as a result of something more than skills. It's strengths in play that set them apart from their peers. Your strengths are areas where you have a potential for mastery and excellence. With some deliberate focus on strengths, you can move your performance from mediocre to good and from good to great.

When we spoke about self esteem, its components included taking a realistic view of your strengths. Buckingham's strengths definition removes from your list those activities or skills you can do, but lack the ability to move them to strengths. It brings life to the phrase "jack of all trades and master of none." Buckingham asserts that telling people they can do anything is not realistic. Initially, I was shocked by his assertion, however after reflection, I agree wholeheartedly with the premise. Encouragement is an appropriate method to motivate youthful exploration. In adults, the "you can do anything" mindset is not realistic and can do more harm than good. Everyone can benefit from the early identification of their strengths.

What's the benefit of using my strengths?

Even though much of the talk regarding strengths occurs in the workplace, strengths can be used to enhance personal effectiveness for individuals and families.

As families develop mission statements, knowledge of each individual's strengths can allow you to align the family member's role around areas that will develop these strengths. Knowing your child's strengths and providing opportunities to put these strengths into play is a great strategy to build their self esteem and to get them started on the right path towards self-revelation.

This same strategy is effective for helping college students select a career. It's so common for students to complete four years of college and still have no idea what they could really be great at. This same student floats into post graduate work or a job that was chosen primarily because it provided the means to repay student loans. By the time this student wakes up, it's ten years later and they have no idea how they arrived at this destination. Knowing your strengths assists you as you set your life goals and plans. Focus on your natural skills and talent for the most fulfillment and satisfaction. Even if reaching your full potential is not your goal, most persons spend a minimum of 60% of their time in a workplace— enjoying 60% of your life makes the effort worthwhile.

Probably the most important benefit of knowing your strengths stems from the fact that we have moved from a skills based, industrial and manufacturing economy to an information economy. The information economy will require many more "knowledge workers."

Developing a strength is impossible without the building blocks of knowledge, skills and abilities.

Coined by Peter Drucker in 1959, the phrase "knowledge worker" describes participants in an economy where information and its manipulation are the commodity and the activity. In the previous industrial economy, an employee was required to produce a tangible product like a car or a plane. In the current economy, the phrase refers to professionals whose value to the organization is gained from their ability to correlate various items of data and external information to create value added knowledge products. For example, it's not enough for a cashier to be able to press a button to ring up the price of the product. The cashier needs to know how to correct any errors in the transaction, address customer questions and provide quality service that motivates the customer to return to the store for additional services or products. In other words, the cashier needs to be smarter than the machine they work with everyday.

Another example is the administrative assistant. In the industrial economy, the main skill was typing proficiency. In the knowledge economy, in addition to the technical skills of typing, the administrative assistant must be proficient in handling confidential information, knowing when to ask questions and preventing interruptions to the manager's schedule. Exposed to information of all sorts, the administrative assistant must know what to do with the information and knowledge that crosses his/her path. It's more than the technical experience, but it's your ability to think as well.

The "right fit" for you depends on your core strengths. To pursue a new role or career without this understanding is to put yourself at risk to leave a career before it gets started. Don't underestimate the value that you place on work. In a recent Associated Press (AP) survey, 91% of the respondents indicated that their jobs are important to their overall life satisfaction. It was so important that 55% reported that they would continue to work even if they won $10 million in the lottery. Fifty five percent is still a shocking statistic. While I would not be in that percentage—it's obvious that great value is placed on our work life.

The "right fit" for you depends on your core strengths.

How do I discover my strengths?

I discovered my strengths by taking the Strengths Finder Profile mentioned in *"Now, Discover Your Strengths"*. The profile results motivated me to begin a much needed transition out of the corporate arena. Other profiles and assessment tools are listed at the end of the chapter. I highly recommend the Strengths Finder Profile. For a 20 minute investment you receive a report of your top five signature themes that have been present since the day you were born. The report also includes a description of each theme. Though the talent descriptors sound familiar, take the time to thoroughly read the descriptions because the meaning is not the common usage of the word. I periodically review my strengths descriptions to keep them on the front burner of what comes natural to me and what energized me.

Even though you have more than five talents, this profile focuses on the most dominant talents and encourages you to build these first. Additional information is available with further analysis. The book has a wealth of information about each of the 34 signature themes and is a very useful reference tool. After I received my report, I was amazed at its accuracy. At first I thought it knew more about me than me, but I later realized that my astonishment was because the profile gave a name to behavior patterns I had noticed all my life. Each time I read one of the descriptions, I had an "aha moment." I remembered saying to myself, "I always knew that about me" or "that's why I didn't like that job." My signature themes resonated with me— I was excited to affirm them because they were truly me. I'm going to share my signature themes with you and show you how I applied them to my current role to make a decision to leave a company for a more fulfilling life and work opportunities. My signature themes are *Strategic, Maximizer, Relator, Positivity and WOO*. (Buckingham's, *Now, Discover Your Strengths*, www.strengthsfinder.com)

For me, being Strategic means I am able to sort through clutter to find the best route. As I sort, I rule out paths that don't lead to my desired outcome. I constantly think about "what if" scenarios and how to avoid getting stuck on an unfruitful path.

When this theme is at work, I am using my unique way of thinking to move through what other people see as confusion and complexity. Based on one scenario, I am able to present several options for your consideration along with the pros and cons of pursuing each alternative. I use this strength to provide "timely direction" in my coaching and consulting practice. As an attorney, I use this strength to provide balanced counsel to families and businesses.

My next strength is Maximizer. As a maximizer, I am fascinated by your strengths. When I meet you, I am unconsciously looking for your strengths. Instinctively—whether you want me to or not—I want to reveal that strength and bring it to the forefront. Whether it's an individual or organization, my natural response is to want to improve its value to you by showing you how to nurture or develop it. I am most challenged when I'm provided the opportunity to cultivate strengths from being a good, to an even greater strength. This strength helped me to select the specific practice areas for my businesses.

The strength of Positivity enables me to bring certain energy to everything I do. It's very hard for me to hide in the midst of a crowd because this strength makes me generous with praise and always looking on the upside. I am passionate and totally engaged in all of my activities. No matter the current circumstances, I always think the future will be brighter for me and for others. It's no accident that the focus of my first book would be about adding value to what you already have and how to maximize that value in your life. My brand identity is action oriented and full of energy. My business logos embody that same energy.

Another signature theme for me is the Relator theme. This theme pulls me toward people I already know. I enjoy developing close personal relationships and understanding what's important to that person. I want others to understand those same things about me and I'm willing to take risks in the relationship to see that this goal is met. I value genuine relationships and conversations. If we are in a relationship, it is important to me that I am able to share in an authentic fashion. If authenticity is not available, I consider you as more of an associate rather than a friend—whether you are friend or family. I have friends that are closer to me than family because of the authenticity of our relationship.On the other hand, I have relatives that are more like associates because of the inability to develop an authentic relationship.

My last signature theme is WOO or Winning Others Over. This strength enables me to enjoy meeting new people. I always see opportunities for common ground with strangers and want to understanding their needs and desires. I am drawn to new people. I'm the person on the elevator who wants to hold a conversation and even makes you forget which floor you were getting off on. In my world, I don't meet a lot of strangers.

I had just accepted an assignment moving me from an experienced HR generalist role to a Recruiting Manager role when I took the strengths assessment. When the assignment was first mentioned, my intuition said, "don't take this role." I had no interest in the role and on top of that, the team members already doing the role, didn't seem that excited about the work. The only intriguing aspect about the position was that it would enable me to develop broader HR skills. With my doubts, I accepted the position, believing I could make the best of any situation. Here's an instance where a strength (Positivity) was overplayed and led me down a bunny trail.

My core accountabilities included mining resume databases for qualified candidates, conducting phone interviews, marketing the company and the prospective role to interested candidates and managing the logistics of the internal interview process.

After taking the profile, and reviewing my core accountabilities, I realized that none of my strengths were fully in play. And while I was desperately trying to be a good team player, it was more than 100% confirmed that this role was not right for me—I would never be able to contribute on any level of greatness in my current role. As a result, it was difficult for me to see any benefit to staying in the current role.

> After voicing my concerns and realizing that the organization's destination for me was unacceptable, it was up to me to choose a different course.

Though I was grateful for the opportunity to develop a new skill, I realized that it was a role I should not have taken. In reality, I left most of who I was at home each day because there was no opportunity to use my strengths in the workplace. After a couple of months of trying new attitudes and telling myself next month would be better, I knew my professional fulfillment was in my own hands and I needed to request a different role.

After voicing my concerns and realizing the organization's destination for me was unacceptable, it was up to me to choose a different course. I used the other strategies discussed in *Now, Discover Your Strengths* to choose my next path. Since that time, I have been able to capitalize on my strengths by choosing work that intentionally plays to my strengths. I absolutely consider whether my strengths will have the opportunity to be used or developed before taking on additional areas. If these alternatives are not available, without regret, I'm able to "say no" to the opportunity. Now, I live, work and play from the inside out—I can authentically be myself. Knowledge is power and it is doubly true in the case of strengths. Armed with knowledge of what you do best and what you can be really great at, you can automatically rule out professions or job opportunities that do not suit your strengths and avoid wasting more than half of your life pursuing careers and activities that don't allow you to use your natural talents for greatness.

Past Experiences and Self Reflection

Depending on your environment, indications of your strengths may have been discovered and developed while you were a child. For others, the discovery of strengths doesn't occur until well into adulthood. The same inward reflection you used to determine your values will benefit you as you discover your strengths. For example, in the last chapter, we talked about reflecting on life milestones to discover values. Take a look at that same milestone chart and reflect on activities that seemed effortless to you. For example, I can look back and see that meeting new people and demonstrating a positive attitude were like second nature to me. I used my past experiences to confirm what the signature themes indicated were my strengths.

Don't forget to consider the significant family relationships that helped to shape you. You can use this same exercise as a starting point to identify your strengths. There are some activities that we always enjoy, no matter whom we are with and when we get the opportunity to engage in them. Focusing on what was actually happening during these activities can point you in the right direction for discovering strength. For example, one of my strengths is winning others over. As I reflect on my teen years, I remember being the person who knew everyone and was always bringing some new person to meet everyone else. Even today, I find myself introducing all of my friends to one another and wanting them to know everyone that I know.

Use the milestones exercise to reflect back on times when you have felt the most confident and satisfied in an activity. Think about what you were doing during that activity and make a list of potential strengths. Other questions might include what has always come very easily for you; what activities did you enjoy the most? Another way to look at it is to ask yourself "what are some of the things I've done in my life that I absolutely would never want to do again?"

Whenever you have an experience that absolutely drains all of your energy, take the time to pinpoint the source of the energy drain. Was it the people who were involved or the activities you were asked to do—in some cases it may be both—whatever it was, you will benefit from knowing what not to get involved in on the next go around. Sometimes a contrasting look can go a long way towards helping you see what you really enjoyed.

Don't be afraid to solicit feedback from others as to what they see as your talents or strengths.

All of these characteristics are clues that you can use to identify talent and strengths in others and yourself. Take a minute to right down as many strengths that you believe you have and hold it for later comparison to other feedback you receive.

Feedback from Others

Objective feedback from others can also provide clues to our strengths. Think about the number of times that someone gave you a compliment you didn't expect. Don't be afraid to solicit feedback from others as to what they see as your talents or strengths. We see ourselves very differently from how others see us. Talk with at least ten different people who know you.

Include people from all environments—family, work, community—get a 360 degree view of what others view as your strong points. Ask each person what they see as your strengths; what do they see you doing really well on a consistent basis.

Keep each list separate and after you have gathered your feedback, compare the feedback lists to see if you can identify any themes. Analyzing your past experiences, getting feedback from others and self reflection will help you to develop a short list of consistent strengths others see in you.

Now, pull out the list you created and compare what you said about yourself to what others said about you. You should begin to see some common descriptors. Combining this information with your Strengths Profile should provide you with a new way to look at your natural talents. This exercise may confirm that the biggest obstacle to being yourself is you! Others will give us the latitude to be who we are, while we spend the majority of our energy trying to hide the part of us that is so obvious to others. We have a limited perspective of who we are. This is precisely the reason why you should not confine your strengths discovery journey to what you think. Be open and receive feedback from others. You may discover a strength that you've overlooked.

The biggest obstacle to being yourself is you!

If you are fortunate enough to find a manager that nurtures your talents, work with that person to maximize the growth opportunity. The best manager I had created opportunities for me to verbalize my thinking and use my strategic strengths. At first I thought she was questioning my analytical skills, but through our discussions she shared that she liked the way I thought about things or my strategic strength in action.

Whether it was a team brainstorming session or simply asking for my perspective, she consistently sought out my opinion as she looked for a direct path to solve her problem. Valuing what her team brought to the table, her goal was to leverage all of the team strengths for better overall results.

Now that I know my strengths, what should I do?

Once discovered, strengths should not be ignored but actively developed. Changing your focus from working on improving weak areas to working on your strengths will feel like a night and day experience. When you work on a weakness, your improvements are minimal and require a substantial investment of time and effort. This same effort could be used to leverage development of your strengths with a much greater return on the investment. Ignoring your strengths is a sure prescription for under achievement. If the usage of natural strengths goes unnoticed, imagine what work would feel like if you had the chance to use your strengths everyday—you wouldn't even notice you were working and you would likely enjoy work more.

> **Ignoring your strengths is a sure prescription for underachievement.**

Understanding and developing your strengths is the key to reaching your full potential. Knowing them brings focus to talent areas that enhance your natural attractiveness. Natural attractiveness permits your core strengths to rise to the surface. If you are willing to invest 20 minutes, you will be able to identify your dominant strengths and how you can develop them. When you add this to the values you identified in Chapter 2, you are well on your way to becoming naturally attractive, our focus for Chapter 4.

Can strengths be overused?

We've spent a lot of time talking about strengths and their benefits. Knowing and using your strengths are essential to reaching your potential. On the other hand, the saying that too much of a good thing can be a problem is also true for strengths. Strengths take you further faster than any other skill or ability you can develop. However, strengths alone are not the full equation of maximizing who you are. Recognizing your areas of opportunities —weaknesses—and adjusting for those areas is just as essential as recognizing your strengths.

It's just as important to develop complimentary skills to support using your skills in the workplace.

Go back to my transition from the generalist to the recruiting role. My intuition was telling me that it wasn't the right role, but my strength of Positivity caused me to believe it couldn't be that bad, so I saw the opportunity to learn something from the experience. And indeed I did learn—don't take roles outside your area of strength—especially if you're a Maximizer. Maximizers like to work in the areas of their strength and believe it's a waste of time to focus on anything else. Mining the database for the right person to contact was more crucial than the actual conversation. While learning the recruiting research skills was initially challenging, that challenge was not enough to sustain active engagement in the role.

It's just as important to develop complimentary skills to support using your skills in the workplace. In many cases, getting to the next level is not only about leveraging your existing skills, but it also includes strategies to not let your strengths blind you to obvious areas that you need to improve in. For example, strength in "thinking" doesn't negate the need for "doing." Most roles require both strengths—it's not enough to come up with the bright idea—you also have to be able to implement the idea as well. Developing complimentary skills brings balance to your strengths and helps you take them to the next level. Taking them to the next level includes being able to maximize who you are in leadership, communications, execution and other development areas. Lois Frankel says it like this:

> "People should not stop engaging in behaviors that work for them, but rather identify the gaps in their repertoire of skills and fill them in with complementary strengths."
> (Frankel, *Overcoming Your Strengths*)

Her philosophy is that you avoid derailing your career by developing strengths and complementary skills. Expanding your business behaviors and skills beyond strengths will give you a much needed edge in today's competitive environment. Her -- their strengths everyday, but still seem to be in the same place.

A balanced perspective includes an understanding of your weaknesses. Weaknesses are your Achilles' heel—that part of you that can derail your forward progress. Your opportunity areas are typically in areas where there is a need to develop complementary skills. Complementary skills are those "gap areas" that we all have. For example, you may be in a role that leverages your strengths, but it also requires you to develop an additional skill that would complement the use of your strength. As a strategic person, this could mean moving from a role where you are an individual contributor to one where you are responsible for leading and developing others.

Your strategic strengths will be helpful as you train others to do the work, but not as important as developing the complementary skill of managing others and accomplishing goals through others. If you continue using your strengths, you will naturally want to complete the work yourself rather than delegating the work and coaching others to meet the same goal.

> "We all have traits, tendencies, and weaknesses that we have long ago labeled "not me," because they were unacceptable to us. When we turn away from those opportunities, we cut off important sources of psychological energy and avenues for growth." (*The 12 Bad Habits That Hold Good People Back*, James Waldroop and Timothy Butler)

Awareness is the key to changing behavior that has a negative impact on your performance. With recognition of the problem comes the opportunity to change and break patterns that are holding you back. Don't allow your weaknesses to become your Achilles heel. They can be minimized, but first must be identified.

Summary

Discovering your talents and strengths are a key component to reaching your full potential. They are the core essence of who you are and have a significant role in determining the quality of your life satisfaction. While extremely important, they are not the total equation. It's always a balanced approach that provides you with the surest foundation. So while you know your strengths and should actively seek out opportunities to develop them, don't overlook your weaknesses. They too provide opportunities for you to stretch and grow in areas that you didn't think were possible. So much of who we are emanates from our childhood and this is no different. Strengths and weaknesses can be ignored or developed. Now that you know, take the opportunity to leverage them both to move you closer to life satisfaction and meaning.

Don't allow your weaknesses to become your Achilles heel.

Key Learnings

*Strengths are hardwired into the core of your being.

*Everyone has strengths and talents.

*Talents can be developed into strengths with application of skills and experience.

Weaknesses can not be overlooked—strengths take you three-quarters of the way and developing complimentary skills in addition to your strengths will take you over the top.

Chapter Four
Natural Attractiveness

"You are fearfully and wonderfully made."
—Psalm 139:14

You've taken the time to get rid of the clutter, define your values and identify your strengths. Now it's time to become naturally attractive. These initial steps have prepared you to begin the transformation process. You are naturally attractive when you affirmatively choose to be yourself. On the one hand, it sounds quite simple; you might even assume everyone has already made this choice. Unfortunately, this assumption is incorrect. Some of your life experiences affirm you, while others make the choice of "being you" more difficult.

You are naturally attractive when you affirmatively choose to be yourself.

This part of the journey reminds me of the Transformers toy. The real objective with the toy was to figure out how to transform it to its "real self." It's an interesting process to watch. The real toy identity is so different from the original it was hard to believe it was the same toy. The first transformation always took the longest to complete. Steady persistence and determination were necessary to figure out the right steps that would reveal the toy's true identity. Once the steps were mastered, you could transform from one identity to the other in no time at all. If you were really good, you could even help others master the steps with other transformers. Even though each toy is different, there were certain keys that worked with every toy.

Life transformation is not quite that simple or as easy as working with a toy. It is similar in one respect—once you figure out which process works for you, it's easy to apply it in different areas of your life and receive multiple benefits. The desired outcome of your transformation is to reveal the real you and allow the world to see your "natural attractiveness." It's who you are when you give yourself permission to be you. When you know, understand and value who you are, your natural attractiveness shines from within and it is contagious. Natural attractiveness goes beyond mere physical beauty, abilities or charisma. Everyone has a uniqueness that makes them who they are. That uniqueness attracts others to you and plays a part in how you view your ability to achieve your potential. Being naturally attractive illuminates a confidence that is contagious and magnetic to others. It's not about what you do, but who you are and the unique DNA that enhances every aspect of your life.

Being naturally attractive illuminates a confidence that is contagious and magnetic to others.

Busy-ness, past experiences and unproductive relationships are dirty filters that keep your natural attractiveness from shining through. Today's culture is occupied with the need to "do rather than be and enjoy." We no longer take time to nurture ourselves or reflect on how we can live more balanced lifestyles. Our life experiences become bigger than life and often become an obstacle preventing us from moving forward. You should value and learn from your experiences and remember that you are not the mistakes or bad experiences—they happened to you, but they are not you.

Another obstacle to natural attractiveness is the perceptions of others and your own self perception. Taking a stand to be you takes courage and confidence. Undoubtedly, you will come face to face with old memories, unresolved life experiences and plenty of emotional clutter. The journey to becoming natural attractive is not for the faint of heart—it's for those who want to achieve their full potential and pursue their life's purpose. It's also for those who want to move beyond their negative self perception and the opinion of others. Natural attractiveness is a lifetime journey with continuous self evaluation and goal setting to actualize your personal mission.

Natural attractiveness requires that you take off the masks that hide who you really are. There's freedom in being able to appreciate and enjoy who you are, irrespective of what the world thinks you should be. This freedom becomes the foundation for reaching your full potential. The motivation for natural attractiveness comes from within. Others may desire it for you, but their desire is not enough to make it happen. Later in the chapter we'll talk about ways that others can support you in your commitment to becoming naturally attractive.

Natural attractiveness requires that you take off the masks that hide who you really are.

Don't be surprised if few seem excited about your transformation. As a matter of fact, on some days, you won't be too excited yourself. Your transformation is going to move others out of their comfort zones. They will have to change their perception of you. You may even feel like turning back—don't! Anytime you move out of a comfort zone or perceived place of safety, your initial reaction will be fear and uncertainty. That's normal—it's part of the journey. Additionally, once you've committed to the course, providence will step in to support you in your efforts. The experience of freedom motivates; anything that hinders freedom will fall away. Anything less than full expression brings conflict to your natural value of self-expression.

Remember the story of the bamboo tree. To the casual observer, from the outside it looks like nothing is happening. Transformation is an inside job. It's changing from the inside out and the result of your individual self motivated efforts. This next stage is providing the opportunity for the new you to take root and become a lifestyle rather than a hobby.

What is self-esteem?

As defined by Webster's Dictionary, self-esteem is "a confidence and satisfaction in oneself." It's knowing that you have limitations, but choosing to accept and value yourself despite those limitations. "Who you are" is comprised of three separate but interrelated dimensions—body, soul and spirit. Therefore both physical and mental attributes are included. The LaBelle Foundation defines self-esteem as "an ongoing process that comes from connecting with your soul and spiritual potential." Self-esteem involves more than fluctuating day to day thoughts. It is the degree to which you approve, appreciate or like yourself. It's based on your attitude about the work you do, achievements, life purpose, potential for success and independence. It also includes an understanding of your talents, natural strengths and weaknesses. It's being able to take a realistic look at yourself and acknowledging while there may be some "gravity issues" which are beyond your control, you value and appreciate your unique individuality. For those issues you do control, its understanding you have the power to choose a different outcome—you can change what doesn't enhance who you are.

No matter how you feel or what you physically see, being naturally attractive is taking full responsibility for working with what you have, changing those things that you can and having a goal that builds on what you appreciate about yourself. You respect yourself knowing that while you aspire to be better, along the way, you won't be perfect. You love and respect yourself as you give yourself room to fail sometimes, take risks and learn from every experience through self reflection. It's moving from reactive perception management to proactive self reflection and values based planning.

How do I get self-esteem?

Everyone arrives in this world with a blank slate of self-esteem. While it is not genetic, self-esteem is a product of your life experiences beginning at childhood. Initially, that primarily includes your parents and immediate family. As you are socialized in other arenas, the sphere of esteem influencers is broadened to include teachers, coaches, neighbors and community institutions. Esteem is developed during your lifetime. Every success, failure, accomplishment and how you are treated comes together to shape your esteem. A steady diet of positive self worth statements will result in higher positive self-esteem. There's a saying that "a child grows as the tree is bent." As you bend a child's development tree, they will grow or esteem themselves in that same way.

Negative or low self-esteem results from harsh criticism, constant ridicule, teasing or even being ignored. Trust is a huge component of good esteem. Anywhere that esteem has been violated there will be a need for a new foundation to support the new you. Target these areas for "esteem building" attention in your goal planning. Finally, watch out for "perfectionism and looking for another's approval." Being perfect and wanting everyone's affirmation robs you of healthy self-esteem. Basing your value on absolute perfection and the approval of others is a no-win situation. It's impossible to achieve and will tear down your existing esteem foundation.

The good news is your esteem can be changed at any time. Childhood experiences can be reversed. Here's a personal example of how my esteem was shaped by a community institution. In the town where I grew up, everyone bought candy, sodas and chips at a small community store. The owner of the store seemed to know everyone in the neighborhood. Before I made my selection, I always asked a lot of questions. I asked so many questions that the store's owner gave me a nickname—Blabber Mouth. I had an immediate negative perception of asking questions and talking to adults. I didn't like the nickname and I avoided going to the store. Hearing the nickname was humiliating to me and really shook my self-esteem.

When I entered school, my teachers encouraged questions and general communication. At that point, I realized talking could be appreciated. As a matter of fact, I was rewarded with excellent grades for talking in class. Since we all like positive praise, going to school became my favorite activity, as you could probably guess.

Self-esteem is a product of your life experiences beginning at childhood.

School was the only place that allowed me to ask as many questions as I wanted without explanation and humiliation. In my case, the store owner didn't know his nickname had effect on me and as I continued in school, he was a great source of encouragement—and he still called me Blabber Mouth until I left for college. However, my response to his nickname was to talk just a little bit more and he even began to ask for and value my opinion. As you work through this chapter, you will remember similar experiences. Start a journal to document the new things you will learn about yourself. Suspend the negative self judgment and make room to change your perception of the impact that the experience had on your life. Now is the time to rebuild and strengthen your personal esteem foundation.

Another aspect of self-esteem is your self image. Self image is how you perceive your physical attributes. A quick look at the plastic surgery and cosmetics industry is overwhelming evidence that today's culture is totally captivated by physical appearance. The need to be accepted for your physical attributes has even produced its own reality TV show. A tremendous amount of emotional and mental clutter is released as the participants begin their journey to a full physical makeover. Many report having been ashamed or embarrassed all of their life regarding some physical conditions. While we can't change all of our physical attributes, there are many avenues available to those who are willing to make a financial commitment.

Every time I visited my best friend's parents' home, they would tell me that my eyes were "so big." I came from a family with big, bright eyes, so no one told us that those big eyes were not to be desired. After hearing that comment, I became extremely conscious of my eyes and even tended to look away rather than at others—hoping they wouldn't notice my eyes. I held a negative perception of my eyes until another neighbor offered a different point of view. I was selling Girl Scout cookies in our small community. When I rang this neighbor's door bell, she said something that totally changed my self image regarding my eyes. She said, "You have the most beautiful eyes; they are so bright and they sparkle so much."

Now that was a change from what had previously been reinforced in my mind. In that instant, the hurt I felt from those comments melted away. At that moment, I accepted that aspect of my physical image. I batted my beautiful, brown eyes at everyone I met and that year, I won the school award for selling the most Girl Scout cookies.

Good self-esteem develops healthy self confidence in who you are and in what you can achieve. It gives you the courage to try new things. You take more risks when you believe in yourself. Even if you have to persist through obstacles, you don't mind.

Even if you fail, you know if you belief in yourself you can recover. You become empowered to make better choices and you know you are capable of following through on your choices. Every part of you is worth caring for and protecting.

Self-esteem should also be realistic, that is, grounded in objective talents, strengths and abilities. In other words, it's ok to believe you can do anything, but realize you can't do everything. If a particular pursuit is beyond your mental or physical capacity, it is unrealistic to continually affirm you can achieve it. Matter of fact, it could lead to the opposite effect—low self-esteem. I'm not referring to overcoming considerable obstacles. Here's an example of what I mean. If your desire is to be a French translator, it's not

self-esteem is a product of your life experiences beginning at childhood.

enough to just affirm your desire. You need to take some action to learn the language. Just saying you want to do it is not enough. Realism is a part of good self-esteem. Positive affirmations are no substitute for good, old-fashioned hard work and initiative.

What is self-efficacy and confidence?

A closely related cousin of self-esteem is self-efficacy. Self-efficacy is your sense of competency and ability in a general or specific area. It's a strong internal drive that repeatedly tells you "you can do it." (Bill Bonnstetter, *If I Knew Then What I Know Now*) It's your belief in your capability to organize and implement action steps to manage prospective situations. Self-efficacy influences the choices we make, how much effort we will engage in, how long we will persist in the face of obstacles. Efficacy is gained by mastery and experience. A person with strong self-efficacy says to themselves, "I believe I can learn how to do a particular activity if I'm given the resources I need to learn."

"It's a judgment of your confidence to complete a specific task. Self-esteem is a matter of being or feeling and self-efficacy is a belief of "I do this."

Confidence to complete a task comes from knowing you have mastered the required skills to complete the specific task or believing you can complete the specific task if provided with the appropriate resources. Just as self-esteem should be realistic, so should self-efficacy. In my experience as a recruiter, three out of four candidates would say they could do any role the company had to offer. While the statement evidenced their confidence in their abilities, it wasn't realistic. Some skills and competencies are transferable, but there are others that require specialized skill and training.

How does self-esteem and self-efficacy impact me?

Earlier, we mentioned the proverb "what you believe in your heart about yourself is what you will become." Your ability to effectively reach your potential is directly impacted by these three areas. It is virtually impossible to achieve your potential if you strongly doubt your ability to achieve meaningful goals. Your strategy to achieving potential should include a realistic assessment of your strengths and a corresponding acceptance of areas for growth. Self acceptance is knowing and understanding who you are and where you came from. It's not forgetting your past, but moving beyond it. The Christian point of view would say, it's believing that God will take good and bad experiences and integrate them in your life in a way that enhances who you are.

If your self-esteem is not solid, you may feel the need to protect yourself from the negative feedback. You will have a perception that you are not important. You might even expect to be cheated and discounted by others. This is not "common sense" but defensiveness designed to keep others away.

Protecting yourself results in a "masking" of the real you. You act happy when you're really not and you live with the constant fear that someone will discover your secret. You seek to please others and at the same time, never feel good enough. Your inner voice constantly belittles you. Finally, you may take on a victim mentality and act totally helpless to change your circumstances and even look to others to take the responsibility. All of these "masks" create stress and anxiety and interfere with your ability to develop meaningful relationships with others. Perhaps you've had the experience of meeting someone who you perceive is very needy. Needy persons tend to drain your energy and emotional reserves.

On the other hand, good positive self-esteem draws others to you. It causes you to be able to build trusting relationships and become independent and autonomous. While the studies differ on the positive outcomes of positive self-esteem, research has shown that "pleasant feelings and enhanced initiative" are two of the benefits. High self-esteem has a definite correlation to happiness, just as low self-esteem has a strong correlation to depression. Everyone wants to feel good—it's our nature as human beings.

Effective self management begins with good, healthy self-esteem. It is the foundation for effectively managing yourself. Other elements of self-esteem include your ability to trust and nurture yourself. Being autonomous allows your identity to grow and develop connections with others. What we believe about ourselves can be the difference between an unfulfilled purpose and reaching one's potential. When we value ourselves and believe in our ability to achieve goals, our self-esteem and self-efficacy support one another to motivate achieving even higher goals. The opposite is true as well, when we do not value ourselves and we doubt our ability to achieve goals, our self-esteem and self-efficacy work have a negative impact. In addition, our feelings of self pity kick in to really make us feel that change is impossible.

How do I improve my self-esteem and self-efficacy?

No matter how your esteem has been shaped, you should take heart in knowing it can be changed for the better at any time. Daily emotional ups and downs are normal due to our fast moving

Don't be afraid to look in the mirror and take note of what you see.

and ever-changing environment. The first step to improving your esteem is a healthy and realistic self awareness. Take the time to become aware of your strengths and areas of needed growth. Don't be afraid to look in the mirror and take note of what you see. Everyone has weak areas that need additional development. Uncovering the weakness is not the problem; it's choosing to live in ignorance or deciding you won't address the area. Self awareness includes deciding on your values and beliefs. You should know what you stand for and have a plan for actualizing your values and purpose.

A most important step is to let go of the past. The neighbors I mentioned in my examples shaped my life in other ways. My relationship with them would have been so different had I not been able to think past what they said. Don't allow yourself to become stuck in unforgiveness and the guilt and shame of past experiences. Reflect on the experience for the learning and then release everything about it that doesn't affirm you. Remember, you are not the experience or the mistake that you made. Be diligent about monitoring your self talk—don't allow it to revert to old memories and negativity—but keep it firmly focused on positive affirmations of the unique and valuable person that you are.

This won't happen overnight, but you can make daily progress toward believing in yourself in a more self affirming manner. "I am somebody!" was first made famous by Jessie Jackson. This simple phrase became the mantra for African Americans as we struggled with cultural self acceptance in the seventies. It was a simple way to sow a seed of esteem into a culture of people who had been told they were worthless since the day they were transported from foreign soil. Some even suggest writing down your positive affirmations, meditating on them and literally visualizing yourself in an improved circumstance. The method doesn't matter as much as taking definite action to improve your self-esteem. Walk in integrity by telling yourself and others the truth and keep your word.

> Reflect on the experience for the learning and then release everything about it that doesn't affirm you.

Another important area is to set goals. You must know what you want to achieve and be willing to direct your energy and choices to achieve the goal. Achieving one goal puts in motion a cycle of achievement that leads to a lifetime of positive growth and achievement. When you don't have a destination, you usually end up anywhere. That might be ok if "anywhere" happened to be a desirable destination—it's usually exactly where you didn't want to be. Setting and achieving goals builds your confidence to try something bigger and more challenging. When goals are specific we know what success will look like. We can visualize when we have attained the goal. Measurable goals help us to appropriately plan from a time and resource perspective. Writing down the goal solidifies commitment and allows providence to step forward in your favor.

No goal is worth setting if you can't take action to achieve it. Achieving your goal is personally rewarding and builds confidence and character. Make certain your goal is realistic and can be completed in a specified time. Unrealistic, ambiguous goals can do just as much damage to your self-esteem as any other negative experience. Other ways to increase your self-esteem include taking responsibility for your choices and actions. Stop the blame game and relying on someone else to rescue you. You are the captain of your ship and it's up to you to take full responsibility. Partner with others who can support you in your journey—that could be your spouse, best friend or professional coach.

In your goal setting, don't forget to plan time for fun, relaxation and taking time to celebrate your accomplishments. Don't wait for the home run to get excited about your progress. You should celebrate every step toward the achievement of the goal. Don't let our all-or-nothing culture keep you from acknowledging small **Don't be afraid to take care of you.** steps. Remind yourself of where you're going by reviewing your goals and how you're going to achieve the goal. Don't be afraid to take care of you. If we totally understood its impact, we wouldn't let a day go by without practicing it—even when we don't think we deserve it.

Some less tangible strategies for increasing your self-esteem include developing a lifestyle of self care that includes affirmation and recognition from others. Don't be afraid to accept or receive compliments from others. Just as you can learn to enjoy receiving compliments, remember an authentic comment can change someone's life. My neighbor's comment about the sparkle in my eyes forever changed how I saw myself. You can make that difference in someone's life. You have to monitor your mental clutter—don't allow those thoughts to accumulate. Get rid of them as they arise. Most are habitual replays of old thoughts and will lessen as you reorient your thinking and beliefs.

Complete a gut check and make sure the thought is not based on some irrational belief like perfection or someone else's approval. Most of all don't forget to set boundaries—don't be afraid to say no. Let others know what you will tolerate in relationships. It's not a no-no to satisfy what's important to you before meeting another's need. As a matter of fact, you may be able to meet their need better if you take care of yourself first. If you need to forgive others, forgive and then move on. Don't get stuck.

Partners in your transition

Enlist the support of friends and others who care about you. Ask them to help you in your process of reestablishing your esteem and becoming naturally attractive. Commitment to this journey may well mean ending relationships and activities that do not support you in a positive manner. Because you are moving out of your old comfort zone, the first emotion you will experience is discomfort. This is natural, don't turn back, but use the discomfort as an opportunity to bring about the change you need.

You may also feel rejected by those who are not ready for you to make the positive change. Don't worry about those folks —they are the ones you really need to leave behind unless they are willing to support you in the journey. Keep in mind, their rejection may not be

Enlist the support of friends and others who care about you.

about you, but really asking the question of what will your changes mean for them. The answer to that question depends on how much of you was not a part of that relationship from the start. Remember, this is your opportunity to be the real you, so don't put on another mask to be you.

If they are not able to enjoy the naturally attractive you, that could be a relationship that needs to change and grow.

It is normal for relationships to change and grow as we change and grow. Remember, you're transforming the structure of your relationships. The desired outcome is to expose them to the real you, the authentic you, the naturally attractive you. The treasure of who you are will come forward and might even encourage them to drop their masks and become naturally attractive.

If you would prefer confidential support, professional coaches are great partners to support you in the initial stages until you want to go public with your journey. You need an objective sounding board to bounce off your ideas. Finally, if your esteem is in a place of pain and overwhelming difficulty, talking to a counselor or therapist could be a better alternative.

Summary

When you work with who you are, you make a decision that you are going to work with "all of who you are—mind, body and spirit. You commit to appreciate and acknowledge everything about yourself and not neglect any aspect. Once you commit, providence moves with you and all sorts of things occur to help you that otherwise would not have occurred. As you commit to work with who you are, expect there will be a whole stream of favorable events that will assist you along the way. In other words, the energy and excitement about being you springs forward. Take full accountability for the transformation and actively pursue your new lifestyle.

Key Learning

 Being naturally attractive is fully accepting who you are—mind, body and spirit.

 No matter how it's shaped, you can take action to improve your self-esteem.

 Self-esteem is realistic and unconditional acceptance of your strengths and weaknesses while maintaining an attitude of worth and value.

 Develop, clarify and embrace a healthy self-esteem and efficacy.

 Adopt a lifestyle of self care. Appreciate yourself daily.

Chapter Five
A Journey with a Destination

*"If you don't know where you're going,
it doesn't matter which way you go."*

—Cheshire Cat, Alice in Wonderland

Introduction

In the first four chapters you cleared the space and identified your strengths and values. You've established a firm foundation to develop your personal mission statement. As extraordinary as it seems, it is possible to fully understand who you are and still lead a life that lacks meaning and purpose. The benefits of your uniqueness will escape you unless you integrate your natural attractiveness into every aspect of your life. It must become habit forming and a lifestyle you feel comfortable in.

Much more than a hit or miss activity, being naturally attractive is an existence born out of discipline and a desire to fulfill your life's purpose. In this chapter, we'll bring it all together to position you to experience a life of meaning and fulfillment. Having a purpose driven life is not just something you read about—it's a lifestyle you have the power to bring into reality. You don't have to ask permission or wait for others to join you. Without a vision or purpose, you're like a piece of driftwood in the ocean being pushed about by the waves of life, without direction and without a destination. You may begin to wonder, "is there more to life?"

Life with meaning and purpose does exist, but it's the result of conscious choices rather than something that just happens to you. Take note of those around you who are living meaningful purpose driven lives. Not one person will tell you they woke up one day to find themselves at a particular destination. Purpose directed lives are a matter of choice and not happenstance. They may not have known the exact path that would lead them to this destination, but they certainly had an end game in mind.

According to *The 7 Habits of Effective People*, written by Stephen Covey, we are to begin with the end in mind. Seeing the end from the beginning gives you the foresight to know what's required to reach the destination. Covey's advice has been repeated by many, yet it's not uncommon to meet people who have not taken the wise advice to heart. Many persons float

Life with meaning and purpose does exist, but it's the result of conscious choices rather than something that just happens to you.

through life without an end game in mind. Because they have no goals, they have no idea where to focus their daily activities.

Without focus, it's easy to wander aimlessly through each day. Appearing to stand still, forward progress is non-existent from day to day. Aimless days are always busy and full of activity, but in the end, there are no real accomplishments. Days become months and months become years. By the time you wake up, your life has passed by and you wonder what happened to your dreams.

Without a doubt, if you don't know where you're going, you'll end up nowhere. That statement is doubly true as it applies to living a meaningful life. If you have no idea of your life's purpose, you'll waste the gift of a lifetime living well below what you could have achieved for yourself and others. When you fail to identify your life's purpose, you choose to deny yourself and others the ability to benefit and grow from your natural attractiveness. It's often what we see in others that motivates us to take action to create significant change in our lives. Your choice to pursue your life's purpose can have a profound effect on you and others around you.

I believe we are all connected and each have a specific purpose that we were created to fulfill. You've been equipped to achieve that purpose and the resources you need are available to you and will come to you as you pursue your life's purpose. St. Augustine said it like this,

> ## "...once you commit, it is as if providence and the universe begin to work with you..."
>
> *Augustine*

Before going further, commit to making a conscious decision to live your best life right now—not tomorrow, not after the children grow up, not when you get around to it—but today. Tomorrow is not promised to anyone and waiting for it to arrive before you live a life of meaning is a risk you don't have to take.

Life has a strange way of bringing unexpected challenges and opportunities. Sometimes, tomorrow never arrives. Today, as you read this book, life is providing you with the opportunity to add meaning and passion to your life by developing a personal mission statement, pursuing your purpose, finding work you love to do and modeling a lifestyle that will inspire others to do the same. You can consciously choose to develop a personal mission statement or continue to live your life based on the mission statement others have developed for you.

A Conscious Choice-Personal Mission Statement

A personal mission statement is an expression of your life's purpose and how you will live out that purpose. Mission statements are specific in what they will achieve, measurable in when they will be fulfilled and tangible enough that others can understand where you are going. Aspects of your values are included, but it is more than a restatement of your core values, it's the what, when, where, why and how of your vision.

Your personal mission statement answers the questions of how you will achieve your life's vision. It's how you will use your core values and strengths to achieve specific goals. You can think of it like your personal constitution, a guiding document that is timeless in the sense that it embodies your natural attractiveness, yet fluid enough to be amended when life's circumstances require changes.

Once established, it's your compass that allows you to take personal leadership of your life. Just by reading the statement, it should provide immediate guidance to cover 90% of the decisions you face on a daily basis. This is true because the statement is the written articulation of who you are and your purpose. If you find yourself faced with the need to constantly review your mission statement, it is too vague and not aligned with your true essence.

A personal mission statement is an expression of your life's purpose and how you will live out that purpose.

The remaining decisions it covers are those tough decisions that require a reminder of why you started down the path in the first place. Mission statements keep the "tough going when the going gets tough." They motivate and inspire you to endure challenges and overcome obstacles. When the rubber meets the road, it's your personal constitution that is the difference between giving up and hanging in there with the belief that your efforts will pay off.

For the big crossroads decisions referring to your mission statement will provide the opportunity to stay focused on a particular course or consciously make a choice to move in a different direction. It's a custom made document with a specific purpose and for your benefit. It's a written expression of who you are and how you intend to impact the world around you. It's both reflective and future focused because it considers who you are from your past experiences and where you want to go.

It's common to hear references to our nation's Constitution, but you rarely hear individuals speak of their personal mission statements. I took a brief survey and asked ten people whether they had a mission statement. If they said yes, I asked them what it was and how were they able to bring that statement to life everyday. For those who did not have a statement, I asked them why not. Those who acknowledged

A personal mission statement is an expression of your life's purpose and how you will live out that purpose.

having a statement, in many cases they had not written their mission statements down, but kept them "in their heads." When asked to articulate their statements, they were unable to do so with any confidence or specificity. Aside from inadvertently irritating some, my desired outcome was to activate their thinking around how the lack of a personal mission statement is impacting their lives.

Those who didn't have a written statement responded they didn't have time to write one, didn't think it was really necessary or didn't feel as if they could control their destiny. From their additional comments, it was easy to hear the telltale signs that they were living without a mission. Whether it was the wrong career, wrong relationships, wrong spouse, no spouse, wrong boss or simply not being understood or valued, each person had the power to change the "wrongs" to "rights" by deciding to take leadership over their responses to life's circumstances.

For those who said they had a personal mission statement, many remembered the process of getting one, but hadn't reviewed it in some time, so though they had taken the time to write one, they couldn't tell you what it was with any more certainty than those who had never taken the opportunity to put it in writing. Here's the learning—writing the mission statement is not enough—implementing the mission is a necessary component.

In the next section, we'll outline the process to develop your mission statement. This discussion will also include strategies to ensure your written statement becomes more than an exercise, but a living breathing document that does exactly what it

Writing the mission statement is not enough—implementing the mission is a necessary component.

was intended to do —provide direction and tangible results.

Every new year, many people start out with resolutions they intend to practice for the upcoming year. Within a month, those resolutions have been discarded or whittled down because they just seem too hard. One way to avoid the guilt of establishing resolutions that you never keep is to take the time to establish a personal mission statement that gives you the opportunity to set some realistic goals. Thoughtfully done, creating a personal mission statement is one of the most powerful and significant steps you take toward becoming the captain of your ship.

Your mission statement makes you personally accountable for the results. Once created, you either have to get busy achieving your goals or figure out what's really holding you back. It is your personal statement of what matters most to you and how you will actualize those priorities. Your mission statement is reflective of your character and your sense of calling or vocation. In short, a personal mission statement is having goals with deadlines— if you can't measure it, it probably won't get done.

At the end of the chapter, I have listed several software programs and online resources that are of valuable assistance in developing your personal mission statement. For those who'd like to start from scratch to begin the journey, here are some simple steps to get you started.

Write it down

Remember those people who carried their mission statement "in their head?" In our chapter on clearing the space, we mentioned that "in your head" is one of the worst places to store something important. A simple, but extremely important aspect of this process is to write your mission statement down on a piece of paper. There's power in the written word and research has shown that people who write down their goals or aspirations are far more likely to achieve them than people who don't write them down.

Once you've completed the process of writing your mission statement, and you have your final version, look for the opportunity to simplify it to an easy to remember acrostic or acronym. Once completed, your mission statement should be easy for you to remember and share with others. Whether it's one word or several pages, the key is to write it down. It's ok to have more than one version of your mission statement—a shorter specific one you can commit to memory and share with others and a longer one that includes specifics and measurable timelines. The more specific it is, the more focused you are in the actions you take to achieve the goals.

Make it challenging but realistic

One reason why resolutions don't have lasting effect beyond January is because they are vague and unrealistic. Ineffective mission statements are those that are too long, too vague, full of flowery clichés and unconnected to your values. The key is not in the length, but in whether the mission statement is really you.

"Success leaves clues."

In other words, is the statement a reflection of you and what you want to accomplish?

Don't write a statement of what you think you should be and then try to build your life around the statement. Build your mission statement around the life you're already living and add some goals that will challenge you to grow and stretch beyond your current abilities.

It has been said that "success leaves clues." Pull from activities where you felt most comfortable and fulfilled in the experience. Earl Nightingale defines success as the progressive realization of a worthy ideal. Anytime you achieved the result you set out to achieve, you've been successful. Look to those successful times for clues to what's most important to you. It's an inside out process just like discovery of your strengths and values.

An effective personal mission statement is short enough that you can commit it to memory, written down so it can be posted in many places and has specific, measurable outcomes. The goal of the mission statement is to provide guidance and motivation to continue forward movement toward your destiny. It's written to help you see through clutter and to propel you and others forward to a specific destination.

Fluid

Personal mission statements are not made to be engraved in concrete and can never be changed or adjusted. Once created, reading or recite your shorter version as a daily reminder of what you want to achieve. Review it quarterly to determine whether you need to make adjustments. Most statements will contain yearly, three year or even five year goals. External factors can bring about the need to adjust some of your long term goals.

Remember this is a living and breathing document—make adjustments along the journey based on your current learnings and experiences. Your initial values and ideas may remain the same, but the path that you choose to realize those values may change. Since change is a constant characteristic of your life, create room to make adjustments based on life changing occurrences.

The Process

As previously stated, there are many ways to approach developing your personal mission statement. Most guides start by reflecting on positive experiences and remembering what things you really enjoy and what activities you enjoy doing. Don't censor your thoughts, write down those experiences whether family, career, friends, relationships, or spirituality. All had a say in shaping a significant positive experience.

As you're looking back, you see themes and connections of what you were doing when you were most fulfilled. This is important to the process because it pushes away the clutter of what others expect from you and asks you to define when you were most happy and excited. Start with at least five positive personality characteristics and describe the way in which you express them. From there, you write down five goals you can associate with those characteristics and achieve within a specific period of time. Initially, since you were brainstorming, you may need to pare down your list or prioritize it to include your two or three most important goals.

Another exercise that is also very helpful in creating your mission statement is to make a list of at least 50 things you'd like to accomplish in your lifetime or things you would do if you won $20 million after taxes in the lottery. There was a time when winning a million dollars in the lottery was a big deal. Recent polls indicate that 60% of the American workforce would continue working even if they won 10 million.

Financial obligations and commitments have a way of limiting our dreams of what we can accomplish. Thinking about what you would do if you had the luxury of doing absolutely nothing is a great way to get at the dreams that mean the most to you. Of course, your first thoughts would be travel and relaxation, but eventually, you'd settle into your new freedom and hopefully a new mindset on what you can now achieve.

Since you've already identified your values and your strengths, you can apply that knowledge to "what you want to do and how you want to express what you want to do." Another area rich with signs of inside out living are your past successes. What have you been successful at over the past few years?

As you look back at your successes, what you really enjoy doing, and your strengths and values, look for themes or connections between them to bring focus to an "inside" area that you can easily live outwardly. Next make a list of ways you can make contributions to your family, your work or business, your community, your faith, your friends or the world in general. As you can see, the list of what you could do has the possibility of getting very long. This is where your values and strengths come into play to bring focus to your list. There will be some areas you can make an immediate contribution to. In other areas, you may need to develop additional skills, experience or contacts to achieve your goal.

Share it with others

In the Holy Bible, the book of Habakkuk makes reference to what happened when Habakkuk received his mission from God. He was instructed to write it down and make it plain, so that others who heard of the mission could run with it. This was good advice for Habakkuk and it is good advice for us as well. We've already discussed the benefits of writing down your mission statement.

When you make your vision or mission plain, you stay away from vague, useless wording that does more to confuse than to clarify. Running with the vision is another way of saying "share the vision with others so they can help you."

We're all connected in some way and just as providence comes together to bring to you those things that support your vision, it includes others that want to help you **"Without a vision** with your mission. As you share your mission, **(mission) the** you undoubtedly will encounter others who have a similar mission and will connect to you **people perish."** for fulfillment of their mission.

In summary, an old proverb says, "without a vision (mission) the people perish." Without a personal mission statement you may find yourself just passing through this journey we call life. To perish means to "disappear gradually"—and that's exactly what happens when you spend your life without an end game in mind. Everyday you disappear into the background of life just a little bit more until there is no memory of you or your contributions.

Designing Your Statement

Ask yourself these questions to jumpstart your thinking as you draft your personal mission statement:

1. What do I want from my life and how will I leave the imprint of my presence with my family, community and work?

2. Write down at least five characteristics you like about yourself. For example, your sense of humor, willingness to learn, creativity, attention to detail, sense of adventure, etc.

3. For each characteristic listed above, describe how you express each characteristic on a daily basis and in different roles. For example, the same characteristic expressed as a manager will be different when expressed as a parent or spouse.

4. Write down five goals you'd like to achieve this year. Make sure they are SMART-E goals; specific, measurable, action oriented, time bound and exciting or energizing. If your goals don't excite and energize you now, imagine how you will feel as you attempt to implement something you're already bored with.

5. Look over steps one through four and prioritize your list by choosing two to three items that are most important to you.

6. Here's an sample from one portion of my personal mission statement: use the following paragraph and fill in the blanks.

> "My purpose is to express my (insert personality characteristics). I will do this by (insert how you will express your personality characteristics).
> When doing these (describe what will result from your actions)"

A portion of my personal statement:

> "I express my sense of adventure in my work
> "by basing my business strategy on creativity
> and innovation. I stay abreast of emerging trends
> in my professions and apply new techniques and
> creative solutions to address client needs."

7. Draft a one paragraph statement that includes specific actions required to achieve your goals. Take your time don't rush for the final product this will become your compass and personal constitution.

8. Once it resonates with you, share it with trusted friends and ask them if it seems to embody the essence of who you are.

9. Reduce the key points of your mission statement to an acronym, for easy memorization. Recite it everyday as a reminder and to focus your activities.

Regularly check progress against your goals and make adjustments when necessary. Take on activities that move you toward the achievement of your life's mission. The other activities belong to someone else's mission—leave those other activities for them—they will enjoy doing them more than you do.

Key Learning

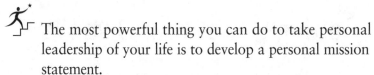 The most powerful thing you can do to take personal leadership of your life is to develop a personal mission statement.

Personal mission statements should be written down and remembered.

Your personal mission statement is your guide to a meaningful living and is a reflection of your "inside out" living.

The most effective personal mission statements are those that are specific, measurable and tangible.

Chapter Six
Getting Out of Your Own Way

"You are your own worst enemy."
—Anonymous

Introduction

When I think about getting out of my own way and what that has meant for me, previous unsuccessful attempts to change some bad habit come to mind. Of course, the memory is not complete without a replay of the feelings of frustration and that taunting voice that says, "See, I told you so, you can't stop."

Fear of failure always comes to the surface anytime you attempt to exchange self defeating behavior for more productive habits. Fear combined with a lack of direction are the primary reasons most goals remain unachieved.

Move beyond your initial fears and look back at times when you were successful in changing some aspect of your behavior. Success is a better starting point for two reasons. First, it's easier to look back and learn from positive experiences and secondly, as we've said before, success always leaves clues.

> Fear of failure always raises its head anytime you attempt to exchange self defeating behavior for more productive habits.

When you look back at a positive experience, your vision is clearer and your focus is not obscured by negative emotions. In addition, positive experiences open your mind and free your emotions to consider the many factors that contributed to your success. Whether large or small, each accomplishment empowers you to work through bigger challenges on the next occasion.

On the other hand, when you reflect on a negative experience, that experience is clouded by your emotional point of view. Even in the face of objective evidence to the contrary, your emotions have a significant impact on how you perceive your ability to change the situation.

It stands to reason, that the same strategies that allowed you to be successful in the past are your blueprint for successful change in the future. Remember, success is doing something everyday to reach your goals. Don't get sidetracked by the mental clutter of society's definition of success—money, power, possessions. Go beyond that definition and remember times where you accomplished simple tasks that were important to you. In other words, we will use the success of the past as the path to success in the future.

As is the case with so many of life's lessons, getting out of your own way permanently is a mentally challenging and on going process. Despite, previous attempts that fell short of your expectations, changing bad habits can be done and applied effectively in other areas of your life. It's like getting a two for one special. Once you

It stands to reason, that the same strategies that allowed you to be successful in the past are your blueprint for successful change in the future.

accomplish the change in one area of your life, it spills over into other areas with very little additional effort.

In the previous chapters, you've spent a considerable amount of time understanding who you are and how you were created to be naturally attractive. Depending on where you were in this journey, living a lifestyle of natural attractiveness may not be that easy.

For some, the journey of the first five chapters was a reaffirmation of what you always knew about yourself. It was a confidence booster that has provided you with a launching pad for blast off toward reaching your full potential. For others, those chapters may have stirred up unresolved issues and the realization that you need a quick course in redeeming the time and getting out of your own way.

What happens when you get out of your way

When you decide to get out of your own way, you take a very powerful step toward creating space for the real you to come forward. The mere acknowledgment that your own actions could be part of the problem is a huge revelation. Just think about how many people you know who lack the self awareness that they are their own worst enemy. It's as if they cannot see what is as plain as the nose on their faces. Wisdom says it like this, "if it were a snake, it would have bitten them." Here's the bottom line, not everyone is aware that they are in their own way. So it's a big deal, when you are able to acknowledge and own the fact that you have a significant role in closing the gap between where you are now and where you want to go.

> When you get out of your own way, you say yes to new habits that allow the best of you to come forward.

When you get out of your own way, you say yes to new habits that allow the best of you to come forward. You give yourself permission to take present action that will not only impact the here and now, but will significantly affect your future. You change the relationship you have with negativity and the constant replay of old messages. You're able to enjoy the here and now without the need to have a perfect future. You lose your self-defeating habits and replace them with productive habits that support an authentic way of life.

Though it may have been slow in coming, your desire to take action now will result in redeeming lost time that resulted from repeating the same behavior over and over. You'll avoid a lifetime of regrets about what your life could have been and will be energized as you are focused on creating the life that you want now and the legacy you want to leave for others.

Focus on the benefits rather than the discomfort. Once and for all, you can let go of the illusion that you can change others and begin to live the reality that there's only one person you can change—yourself. You can let go of the excuses that keep you on a treadmill of self limiting behavior and give yourself permission to change. The more you practice and believe that you have the ability to change this behavior, the easier it becomes to break free of self defeating habits.

When you are bombarded with mental images of how difficult it's going to be, remind yourself of the benefits you'll experience as a result of working through the difficulties. Focus on the benefits rather than the discomfort. It has been said that when the misery of the current situation outweighs your fear or comfort of moving forward, you'll have the motivation you need to get started.

Of course, you can always wait until you are at the end of all of your efforts and emotionally drained; but why not use your energy for something more worthwhile. Seize the opportunity to climb up the ladder of accountability and move from victim to being master and commander of your ship—the ultimate power position.

With this position comes the ability to respond and make choices based on your desired outcomes rather than making knee jerk reactions to emotional and external stimuli. For example, prior to starting my consulting practice, I knew I was dissatisfied with my current position and I could identify at least ten reasons why I felt the way I did.

None of the reasons pointed back at me—matter of fact, many of the reasons revolved around other people and their actions toward me. As I look back, I can hear myself blaming others for something I had the ability to change. As I sat on my fence of indecision, being very vocal about my dissatisfaction with the current state of affairs, I was comfortable holding everyone else accountable for my lack of initiative.

Matter of fact, when my husband had heard enough about the problem and what I knew to be the solution to the problem, he asked me why wouldn't I just take the next step. He had heard me whine about it for ten months, so he clearly understood the problem and could see where my vision had become clouded with emotional baggage. Each week, I'd tell him what I was going to do and then find myself not doing those things as we sat down to have dinner the next week. I had developed a strategy to solve the problem, but I wasn't taking action.

My indecision went on for a few months and took over every bit of my conscious thinking. Indecision has a paralyzing impact. Not only are you in limbo on that decision, the mindset spills over into other areas and can become unbearable. I literally couldn't do anything. Finally, my husband pushed me over the edge by putting his foot down. In no uncertain terms, he said to me, "you need to leave that job so that the rest of us can have some peace."

Though I knew it was true, hearing it from him seemed to give the statement its own life. After my initial shock at his frankness, it was clear I needed to submit my resignation as soon as possible. This mentally checked out state was not only driving me crazy, but the rest of my family as well. It was as if my dual mental state had been exposed and since it made absolutely no sense, the only choice I had was to rid myself of the duality.

The moment I decided to take the next step, it was as if I had dropped a 100-pound weight. Acting on the decision became easier after I resolved it in my heart and understanding resigning was the right choice for me. I let go of fear, others perceptions and the feeling my choice was a win or lose proposition. The chains had finally been broken. I was breaking free to pursue a life of my own choosing.

Not only was it liberating, but it was so essential to my continued forward progress. It was liberating to know I was in control of the very thing that was holding me back. I had the keys to my own freedom. Once you make the decision and begin to share it with others, it's amazing how many persons will try to talk you out of a decision that took you a long time to make. If you're not certain of your decision, you'll consider turning back when you share your vision with others.

How could I be in my own way?

You are in your own way when your allow anything to limit your natural attractiveness. Negative self talk, emotional roller coasters, procrastination and perfectionism, seeking approval from others, and failing to forgive are just a few self defeating behaviors. It's not my intention to provide an exhaustive list, but some practical considerations regarding some of the more prevalent obstacles. What specifically holds you back is personal to you; it's not the same for everyone. Even when it's the same barrier, the manifestation of the obstacle is different when you consider individual upbringing, personalities and life experiences.

What is easy to you to overcome can be very difficult for the next person to work through. Consider this possibility when you feel the need to questions the actions of others. Not everyone is like you. What comes natural to you can be difficult and challenging to the next person. The important thing is to identify the barriers and implement strategies to stay out of the way.

Negative Self Talk

Continually hearing messages that remind you of your perceived inadequacies and failings can prevent you from establishing a new image of yourself. Your mind is the most powerful resource available to you as you embark on changing any behavior. Your belief about whether change is possible is a formidable obstacle that must be overcome. The Holy Bible recounts Jesus saying to his disciples, "All things are possible to those who believe." If you don't believe you can change, nothing in this book will convince you otherwise.

In addition, we are usually tougher on ourselves than others are. Our tendency to magnify negative experiences and equate them to who we are is a very short stretch. Our first response is to immediately judge our actions as something only the biggest fool would have done and therefore, that must be me. This negative self talk squeezes out the possibility of learning anything from the experience.

Unforgiveness and Holding Grudges

This is probably one of the more deceptive barriers to personal growth and development. It pretends to be directed at others, but its very essence is to hold you captive to its effects. While it may be a virtue to forgive and forget, it's not a virtue that is easily attainable without considerable struggle. When we fail to forgive or hold a grudge, it is tantamount to continuing to blame others.

We are usually tougher on ourselves than others are.

We blame others when we are not yet ready to take action to bring resolution. At times the mental desire to forgive exists long before forgiveness may be able to authentically manifest. You know in your heart you need to forgive and let go, but the emotions that accompany your pain are too strong to overlook.

Unforgiveness does more damage to you than to the person it is directed at. It is mentally draining and hides itself well until you see the object of your unforgiveness. Suddenly, your experience with this person can come rushing back with unexpected emotional impact. You may have convinced yourself that you had resolved this situation, only to find that unforgiveness had simply found a convenient place to hide.

Looking for Approval

When you look for the approval of others you automatically relinquish the driver's seat and give control of your life to another. It's a no win situation due to constantly changing expectations that require repeated approvals. In addition, there's no chance that your natural attractiveness will be allowed to shine through.

> **Unforgiveness does more damage to you than to the person it is directed at.**

Those who have overcome this particular obstacle will tell you that rarely is the approval you seek given or worth the continuous proving that one has to engage in to maintain the approval. This is particularly problematic when the person from whom we seek approval is someone we love, like a parent or spouse. In some cases, professional therapy may be necessary ingredient to break through.

Perfection

Failing to give yourself room to learn from a mistake is the self defeating behavior of perfection. Don't allow life to become a constant exercise in doing everything right the first time. This doesn't mean you neglect proper preparation, but it does mean that with that preparation, you expect learning as a part of the process.

Life is a continuous learning process and will never be without mistakes. It's human nature to make mistakes along the journey; that's why we call it life and it's exactly the reason why everyone's journey is different. The journey is about our experiences and what we gain from them.

We stop learning when we stop living. The race of life is not given to the swift or to the perfect, but to those who stay in the journey until the end, mistakes and all. Mistakes and imperfections are God's way of making sure that we stay in touch.

Procrastination

Procrastination is avoiding a task that you know you should complete. Just as the other behaviors are habits, so is this one. It's not a fatal flaw and it can be overcome. It was hard to overcome, but you are reading this book today because overcoming procrastination is achievable with diligence and persistence.

We stop learning when we stop living.

Procrastination interferes with your personal and professional success because it is the result of poor time management, unrealistic expectations, perfectionism, fear of success or failure, distractions, boredom, negative thinking and the list goes on.

To overcome procrastination, begin by setting realistic goals based on your priorities. There is a finite amount of time that's available for each day. Spend your time on your most important priorities. Change your attitude about how you will approach getting things done. Instead of telling yourself you have to finish the entire project, break it down into manageable tasks.

Learn to tolerate the discomfort that results from replacing habits that break procrastination. Forgive yourself if you find yourself slipping back, but do continue to try again. At the end of the day, it was the support of my family and writing coach that pushed me through to the end. I can still hear my coach saying, "Stop thinking about it and write it...get over your need to know everything there is to know on a subject." It was during those times I realized I was really making the writing harder than it needed to be.

Blaming Others

It's very easy to blame others when we are not experiencing the life we want. Your natural response is to look externally for reasons why progress is not being made. When you blame others for what doesn't exist in your life, you have truly abdicated any semblance of ownership and accountability for your own poor choices. The blame game is easy to play, but hard to win.

If you are intent on having a life of meaning, at some point, you have to face yourself. No real progress can be made without a reality check. You must ask yourself what role did you play in arriving at this destination? The answer to that question may bring feelings of regret, guilt, anger and a host of other negative emotions. But those emotions are the precursor to building a stronger foundation on which to move forward.

> If you are intent on having a life of meaning, at some point, you have to face yourself.

What do I do to get out of my way?

There are *five steps* to getting out of your own way. Each step builds on the previous one and requires your full commitment to overcoming self defeating habits.

Step One: *Become more self aware*: Self awareness encompasses the physical as well as the mental arenas. When we feel anger or some other emotional response, we actually have a physical sensation that accompanies these emotions. Pay attention to the times when the self defeating behavior tries to manifest.

When I am overwhelmed and have deadline pressure, my mind goes through a mental checklist of all of my commitments and reminds me that there is no way they can all be completed. It convinces me I have to do everything rather than prioritize and complete what's most important.

As I became aware of this mindset, I was able to develop strategies to neutralize its impact. Now, I slow down and remind myself of the "must dos" for the day that need my direct attention. I then look for opportunities to have other team members complete some of the tasks. In some instances, some activities are permanently deleted because they should not have been on the list anyway.

In other words, when I slow down and get off the treadmill, I'm in a much better position to reflect on my actions rather than respond to the loudest squeaking wheel. My attention goes to the priorities rather than the activity that cries out for the most attention.

Step Two: *Be persistent and forgiving*: Bad habits don't disappear overnight. Overcoming self defeating behavior is something you work on everyday. The more physical, mental and emotional awareness you have regarding the behavior, the more likely you will be able to nip the behavior in the bud. Give yourself at least half the time it took to develop the habit.

It won't take nearly that long. Matter of fact, experts suggest that you can change behavior during a 21–30 day time period. That's a wonderful motivator, but you and I both know that for practical purposes, the 21 day solution only works when you're on vacation. Begin with an attitude that the changes won't be instant and give yourself permission to grow into the new behavior. Your mental attitude is just as important. Believing you can do it is more than half the battle. Take down the mental roadblocks and visualize yourself overcoming the behavior.

Step Three: *Count the costs.* Before you take action, do a brief cost/benefit analysis. Consider the consequences of engaging in the behavior and what you will likely have to give up if the behavior continues. A more positive motivator is to visualize what you will gain by changing your behavior. Sometimes the full impact of our behavior is immediately apparent. Short term thinking can result in long term consequences.

Step Four: *Develop alternative behaviors*: Once you raise your self awareness and commit to staying the course, you can lighten up and go easy on yourself if you find yourself repeating the same conduct. Counting the costs has two effects; it brings to the forefront the short and long term consequences of not changing the behavior. It also gives you the reflection time you need to brainstorm alternative paths.

Visualization is a powerful tool to change your opinion of what's possible to achieve. In the New Testament of the Holy Bible, believers are encouraged to call those things that are not as though they were. In other words, you can speak a different outcome into existence by saying that it is so. Visualize yourself successfully overcoming the self defeating behavior and replacing it with productive, life transforming behavior.

Step Five: *Reward every step.* Don't wait for the home run to reward your efforts. Be grateful for every small step of progress. Life is a game you learn to play more effectively everyday. There are days when you are propelled forward by a giant home run and other days when your progress could be characterized as a base hit or a bunt. Whether a home run or a base hit, take the time to acknowledge the progress and be grateful for the opportunity to begin again on another day.

Key Learnings

Self awareness is the key to getting out of your own way.

Your self defeating behaviors are unique to you.

Be persistent and less critical of yourself.

Celebrate and reward yourself as you make progress.

Chapter Seven
Maintaining Natural Attractiveness

"Be yourself, that's all there is of you."
—Ralph Waldo Emerson

Introduction

We are close to the end of our journey together and at the start of your walk toward maintaining your natural attractiveness. It's a journey worth continuing as you pursue reaching your full potential. The more you live as your authentic self, your desire for authenticity will extend into every area of your life. It's up to you to make the daily choice to live authentically and express your natural attractiveness. You must decide to be the captain of your ship and live your best life now rather than waiting for a more opportune time.

The ever changing lifestyle of the American culture will provide many opportunities to return to superficial living. Constant activity and busy-ness will continue to pull you away from reflection time. Staying out of your own way and enjoying the here and now must become disciplines that are practiced everyday. Reflection time is more than a hobby, it's a strategy for maintaining authenticity. Take the opportunity to learn from life and your shortcomings. Let courage become your friend as you adjust your behavior on the way to maximizing your potential.

This chapter will take a holistic approach to review key areas that are essential to maintaining your natural attractiveness. Armed with knowledge of your hard wired talents and a solid understanding of your values, you are well on your way to pursing a life and career of meaning and significance. Keep the clutter clear; don't let clearing the space become a one time activity. You paid a price to rid yourself of the clutter. Ensure that you get the biggest return on your investment by logging time for maintenance cleaning in all of clutter's hideouts. Keeping the clutter out supports your lifestyle that is aligned with your values and priorities.

Gone are the days of seeking the approval and permission of others to be who you were created to be. As a result, your interactions and relationships with others are enhanced by your desire to be the best of who you are. Every sphere of influence gets the best of you. The unique wiring that makes you who you are is to be shared with others as you maximize your potential.

Live out your Personal Mission Statement

Don't just create a personal mission statement; live your mission with passion and energy. Be decisive about the footprint you leave in the earth. Be the author of your own epitaph; continually ask yourself whether your life is a living example of that epitaph. It's your internal navigation system to keep you on track. Update it every year to ensure you can arrive at your desired destination. My personal navigation system has as it's onboard guide my Christian beliefs. My faith and mission statement guide me through the crossroads decisions.

Stay Connected to Your Authentic Self

Now that you know "who you are," take the time to stay connected with your authentic self. Natural attractiveness is not a destination, but a constant process of growth and development. Be deliberate about making time for yourself. For me that means almost daily journaling. It's still a labor for me to write everyday—but I'm happy with writing just a little everyday. It really keeps me sane and conscious of areas that are trying to get out of control.

Discover what helps you to stay connected and incorporate it into your lifestyle. Writing is my time to gain self awareness about my emotions and anxieties. It is so effective at focusing me that I write as I pray. My writing time is my reflection time. It's also my time to be authentic with myself about me and how I'm working out my stated values with my family and others.

Flex Who You Are

Flexing is adjusting your behavior to those around you. It is intentional behavior designed to increase your effectiveness in communication, relationships and productivity. You flex every-day, it is a natural and intentional response. Natural flexing occurs when you meet someone who has similar values, beliefs, personality and behavior style. It's easier to adjust, it's slightly different, but not so different that the adjustment challenges you.

Intentional flexing is a choice—sometimes you do and some-times you don't. Knowing who you are is not a license to force your natural attractiveness on others. Who you are is a gift to be shared with others and you have a reciprocal obligation to be open the natural attractiveness of others. So flexing is not optional — it's a requirement of effective and productive living.

When you notice a disconnect, flex to meet the needs of your audience. It's not a change to the content, but a change in style and delivery to enable your audience to "hear your message." It's the opposite of the Golden Rule. The Golden Rule says that you should "do unto others as you would have them do unto you." Treating others like you want to be treated works well if everyone else is like you.

Without a doubt, you will meet individuals who are exact opposites of you in terms of how they receive and process infor-mation from their external environment. It's as if every commu-nication with them is a strain—none of your natural flexing works. If you don't have the skills to adjust your interpersonal communication skills, the strain can cause you to avoid contact with that person. The goal of this book is to have you share your natural attractiveness, not to hide it from others.

The Platinum Rule states that you should "do unto others as they desire to be treated." This is the better communication rule. It goes without saying that not only do you want to be heard, but you want others to listen to your message and receive it's contents. Have you ever listened to a speaker that was down right boring? You heard their message with your ears, but did not listen to their message with your heart to receive it.

Every speaker has a specific message that comes from within, but it is up to them to adjust the delivery of the message for maximum listening impact. People won't hear you just because you have something to say. People hear you when you speak their language. The best relationships are identified by excellent communication skills, flexibility, and mutual respect. All of these skills are greatly enhanced as you style flex.

Your ability to communicate is so important that it has been said "if people around you will not hear you, fall down before them and beg their forgiveness, for in truth you are to blame." If others cannot hear our message, it is not their fault but our own for not adjusting the delivery of our message to meet their ears and understanding. Justice Louis Brandeis is quoted as saying,

"Nine-tenths of the serious controversies which arise in life result from misunderstanding."

Poor communication causes problems for everyone. It impacts personal and team productivity, interpersonal relationships and leadership abilities.

Lead as you are

Every person has the opportunity to be a leader. From the youngest to the oldest, from kindergarten through retirement we have opportunities to lead others. Ahsha, my oldest daughter had her first slumber party when she was four years old. She invited six little girls over for an evening of fun and socializing.

After everyone had arrived, these seven little girls, on their own accord, sat down in a circle and said the first decision for the evening was "who's in charge?" Even at an early age, we expect others to step up and lead. One by one, each of them declared, "I'm in charge!" Twelve years later, each one is still in charge and very independent in the path they have chosen for themselves.

Every person has the opportunity to be a leader.

Sometimes we lead others in the pursuit of a specific goal for a particular group and other times we lead others in pursuit of a personal goal. Whatever the outcome, everyone has the potential to become a leader. What you believe about your ability to lead can have major impact on what you believe you can achieve in your lifetime. What we believe in our minds is such a powerful thing—yet our beliefs are not always based on truth. You may have the ability to lead, but if you believe that leadership is not for you, you will never lead.

We are the captains of our ships and we can choose whether to lead or not. Leadership is defined as the ability to influence others. With this simple definition, it's easy to see how every person has a sphere of influence and leadership. True leadership is knowing who you are and leveraging your ability to influence others in a positive fashion.

Leadership doesn't mean you pursue your personal goals only. Leadership includes your ability to pursue goals that are important to others and to pursue careers and livelihoods that interest them by exposing them. It's true, not everyone will be a leader like President Clinton, Muhammad Ali, Mahatma Gandhi or even Mother Teresa, but everyone has the ability to influence in their arena and should take the opportunity to do so.

Maximizing Who You Are

Our culture measures whether we have reached our full potential in terms of what we have attained. Substantial monetary wealth, real estate holdings, mansions and estates are indicators of a successful life. Quite naturally, the inverse—lack of material wealth—indicates a life that did not reach it's potential.

Our culture's perspective may not change during our life; however, you can change whether material wealth is the yardstick you use to measure whether potential has been achieved. Material wealth has many sources; reaching one's potential in nine out of 10 cases is not the cause.

Reaching potential is the intersection of knowing your strengths, passions and values and consistently making choices based on that knowledge. It is that simple. As humans, we are perplexed with simplicity. We don't understand it, nor do we believe that simple is better. We struggle with the feeling that anything worth having should be borne out of great struggle and complexity.

Our past experiences of progress have been at the hands of great sacrifice and so we believe that to be true even when we've learned it to be different. And that's the beauty of maximizing who you are. It's so simple. It's being you from the time you open your eyes in the morning until you lay your head down at night. It's freedom from manipulating situations and allowing others the same freedom to be themselves. I know it sounds too simple, but it is one of the reasons that motivated me to write this book.

It was so hard to be what everyone else wanted me to be. There was a constant pressure to measure my life's achievements by an artificial standard. My "aha moment" occurred when I decided I would just be me all of the time and see how it worked. I can't describe the immediate sense of freedom that poured over me as I really understood what I was saying to myself. It was a two step process. First, I discarded everyone else's standards and secondly and most importantly, I began to create, develop and implement my own life standard.

For the first time, I felt completely accountable for what happens in my life. I wasn't waiting on my employer, my church, my family or even my husband to deliver my personal fulfillment. I literally said to myself, "Denise, you're accountable for this life; it will be what you make it."

It brought to mind a conversation I had with a boss who I knew did not support me and did everything she could to minimize my existence in the organization. My interactions with her became superficial and quite stained. Instead of moving away from one another, every contact we had became a test of wills. In one encounter as we were pretending to have a conversation, it became crystal clear I was being tolerated rather than nurtured. To stay where you are tolerated is a waste of time. Literally, this means your uniqueness is not valued or appreciated in that place. At the end of the day, I resigned from the position and never looked back. I took up the mantle of living a life of my own choosing.

Instantly, I felt like the question of my life's purpose would be answered during this journey. My passion for moving to this new place grew daily. Everyone close to me could see the change— it wasn't physical, it was mental. My attitude about where I was going was excitement rather than fear and uncertainty.

Maximizing potential is one of those phrases you see everywhere. You know you're supposed to do it, but you don't know what it is or how to accomplish it. Merriam Webster's dictionary defines maximize as "to make the most of." That same dictionary defines potential as "existing in possibility." Let's restate the question: How do I make the most of my existing possibilities? "Making the most of" involves knowing your desired outcome and pursuing every opportunity to get closer to that outcome. It is having a mindset that doesn't rest on a current success, but is consistently open to realizing another possibility.

Look at the life of George Washington Carver. He made the most of the peanut—he maximized the peanut in over 300 ways. He was able to see what the peanut was capable of being, but had not become. In other words, his mind was open to yet another use for the peanut.

Even though he didn't see all 300 ideas at one time, he didn't allow his mind to become captive to what he already knew about the peanut. As human beings, we instinctively see what we believe. If we believe we can see more, we do—if we believe we won't see more—we don't. An old proverb says it like this: "be careful what you allow into your heart, it is the wellspring of life."

You may not be able to come up with 300 ways to maximize who you are; but certainly you can change your mindset to expect that there's always more than what you can see with your natural eyes. Don't allow life's quick pace to channel you toward one dimensional thinking. Try not to hold too tightly to one specific outcome. The new outcome you're avoiding could be number two on your list of 300 ways to maximize who you are.

When I speak at Career Day at my daughter, Thobi's fourth grade class, I ask the students, "which area of practice would you like me to focus on—attorney, coach or author?" Every time, the answer is "all three." For their classes, I represent the individual that has a desire to accomplish many things in their lifetime and believes you should pursue each opportunity. I am a passionate advocate of pursing natural attractiveness in every sphere of influence. I tell others, "you can pursue more than one profession and be great in any arena that involves your strengths."

Without fail, I get emails from 4th graders who are excited to know they can be more than one thing and don't have to choose between two things they are passionate about. Planting a seed to expand the possibilities is an important contribution I enjoy making.

The saying "timing is everything," is so true. The window of opportunity is not open forever; it opens and closes during different seasons of your life. Distractions, inflexibility and just down right hard headedness can cause you to miss your season of opportunity. Before your window closes, wake up to the possibilities.

Having the power of choice moves you from victim to empowered individual. In reality, that movement is really not a great distance, but in our minds, it can seem like a mile long chasm. You can choose another course for your life during those windows of opportunity. Perhaps crossing the chasm is not the way to go, but dealing with what created the chasm could be the solution to the problem. Sometimes the thing, you are trying to avoid is the very issue that should be dealt with before moving on to the next place.

Finding Work You Love

It is a myth that you can't find work that you love doing. There are many people who go against conventional wisdom and pursue work that provides personal and career satisfaction. Some have gone so far as to say, "do what you love and the money will follow." That's radical thinking for the 75% of American workforce that's not excited about the work they do everyday.

Although probably not true, it certainly seems like the 75% of the persons that don't like their jobs are usually in front line customer focused positions. It's the person at the retail counter who never looks at or acknowledges you—they just put your change in your hand. They are the people at the drive-thru window who just don't care whether your order is correct. You've met some of these people and many others. After your encounter, you scratch your head and say, "they must have gotten up on the wrong side of the bed" or "they are having a bad day" or "they are in the wrong job." It is not a myth. It is entirely possible to find work you love and get paid for doing that work and bringing a standard of excellence to it. The next time you notice someone who enjoys their work; take the time to ask questions about how they arrived in that particular arena. Listen for opportunities to adopt their success strategies and apply them in your life.

Empowered and Focused:
Your Personal Brand Strategy for Success

Since the average working life now last some 50 years, effectively managing your career is a whole new ballgame. The old paradigm of allowing the company to "brand you" and delegating your destiny to the hands of others is unacceptable for the 21st century career professional.

According to Peter Drucker, today's work economy requires every individual to stay alert and fully engaged in knowing when and how to change the work that they do. No longer is the goal to become an expert in a particular area; but the desired outcome is to develop portable skills that can be carried to the next playing field.

Whether you're in a public or private sector position, continually seek out opportunities that allow you to leverage your strengths and internal expertise and are aligned with personal and organizational goals. Every American worker needs to create their own personal brand strategy for success.

Here are ten key areas to consider in developing your personal brand strategy. Your strategy can become a subset of your personal mission statement.

Expand your self-awareness

Within a company's culture, it's not unusual to have your value to the organization based on a superficial standard of "how well does she/he fit in." While common place, this limiting standard fails to consider your strengths and talents. To have your unique strengths included in your value proposition, you must know what they are and be able to articulate how you can use them to impact the company's bottom line.

Make sure you know more about you than your organization knows about you. Resist the temptation to wait until someone else notices to develop a complementary skill in a developmental area. It's your accountability to have a full understanding of the value you bring to the organization and promote that value with key leaders.

Pay attention to opportunities to help your manager or coach manage you in a way that stretches you and maximizes your strengths. It's not just about promoting yourself; it's about improving the ways that you work best, knowing where you fit within an organization and how you can best contribute to organizational objectives.

Most importantly, your self knowledge will reveal to you areas where there's a need to develop complementary skills and where you may have no skill at all. There are many stories of career derailment due to project leadership in an area where the individual lacked the requisite strengths to complete the project according to company objectives.

Become proactive and address these areas before they derail your career progress. Leverage performance appraisals and developmental discussions to ask for your company's support and resource to continue your professional development.

Develop new networking skills

Just a few years ago, when one used the word networking, the mental image of "sucking up" may have come to mind. Whether you enjoy it or not, networking is a part of every landscape. It is critical in the business, personal and community arenas. Networking is the mutual exchange of ideas and information that enhances your knowledge and experience and benefits all involved.

Expand your networks to include a cross section of the community in which you live. Since all cultures are not afforded the same networks within an organization expand the demographics and diversity of your key contacts. Be a bridge and open the networking door for someone who may not have a full network available to them.

Facilitate new networks by bringing others together who have complimentary businesses to build new relationships. Instead of keeping your good news to yourself, share what's going on with your progress on key projects with your mastermind group. If you don't already have one, build your own team of five to seven trusted advisors outside of your current organization, but who have achieved a level of success you are looking to attain.

Develop flexibility in attitude and career choices

The current knowledge economy is one of constant change and if flexibility does not come easily for you, you may find yourself being labeled as hard to work with or work for. If your strengths are in problem solving, be careful to build trust before you identify weak areas in a co-worker or partner's proposal. Before objecting to a course of action, always seek to understand. Be willing to consider many options as long as the desired objective can be reached.

Flexibility is not just for attitudes; it's for career choices as well. Since we have moved the paradigm from functional expertise to portable skills, be willing to consider any role that will allow you to leverage your strengths and make significant contributions. Typical career progression is no longer a straight path, but more of a matrix of opportunities designed to develop your leadership abilities. Stay in the driver's seat; leverage your self-awareness to align your strengths to current or upcoming leadership needs within your organization.

Walk the talk

When what you say matches how you live, others say that your life demonstrates integrity. Walking the talk is the expression of your integrity. One barometer of your current level of integrity is the feedback of others. You should know the precise state of your brand within your sphere of influence and community. Passive ignorance is not an excuse. If you've had some bruising experiences, evaluate the situation and create a strategy to refocus the image of your brand. It can be done. We've seen it done with products all the time. Just when we thought there was no way to revive the brand, constructive, objective feedback was just the catalyst that was needed to provide the energy to make the changes.

Receiving feedback is easier when you remember that feedback is a gift. Now is not the time to develop sensitivities; you don't have to agree with the feedback—just act on it. If you're uncertain, ask your mastermind group for input. The point of feedback is not the destination, but a stopping point to develop deeper skills to prepare for the next stop on your journey. Be grateful to have a 360 perspective of your brand's image.

Leverage your communication and interpersonal skills

Every successful person has honed their ability to develop relationships and communicate their message. These so called "soft skills"—building relationships, collaborating with others, and developing interpersonal competence—are the critical entry ticket to the playing field in the knowledge economy.

Learn to play well with others and get things done through others. Project self confidence despite what the organizational environment may say to you. If this is an area where you need improvement, seek out a corporate coach to help you step up your skills in this area.

Be Nurtured and not Tolerated

As you may be aware, there are certain work environments that seem to bring out the best in you. You're engaged in the work that you do, excited about your contributions and a valued asset to the company. Stay with companies that appreciates and values what you bring to the table. If you find yourself in an organization where your contributions are being tolerated, begin planning a strategy to reposition your brand.

Being tolerated is a powerless and undesired position. It takes you off your game and puts you in the position of constantly proving your worth to the organization. Seek out feedback to understand where your shortcomings are. If there's an opportunity to change the internal perspectives, do all you can to make a positive shift. In some cases, the only alternative is to plan an exit strategy. Exiting from a powerless position is always a better option than staying where your talents and strengths are not appreciated.

Remember the 80/20 rule

Become an 80/20 individual. In his book, *The 80/20 Individual,* Richard Koch provides timeless guidance on how to build on the 20% of what you do best. Focused on accomplishing more by doing less, Koch believes that the world belongs to individuals who leverage the Pareto Principle.

Named after its originator, Vilfredo Pareto, the Pareto Principle states that 80 percent of results flow from 20 percent of causes. This principle enabled Japan to grow faster than any other industrial nation between 1957 and 1989. From an individual perspective, Koch shows you how to create wealth and improve your well being.

"The 80/20 principle enables anyone who is determined, bright, and hardworking to stamp a footprint on the world."
— Richard Koch

Don't let the 80% of minutia take over your life; focus on the 20% that includes your strengths, talents and priorities that bring 80% return. Work with who you are and what's working in your environment. You'll see an exponential increase in productivity as you refine your focus.

Closing Summary

Living a life of your own choosing is an intentional activity. It doesn't just happen. It's a challenge to wake up everyday deciding you are in control of your destiny. I freely admit, there are some days when I don't want to be in charge of my destiny. On those days, I believe I would really like it if someone else would take control. And for those days, we have family, friends and others who support us through tough times. These are also the times to draw on the energy reserves you build up by spending time for you. When I feel this way, I know I need to get away from everything and relax. I need to let everything go—just for a moment and regroup.

It's amazing what a little time out can do for you. We think it is good for our children, but we rarely think about it being good for adults. Whenever you feel overwhelmed and seem out of control, take a time out. The purpose for the time out is to slow down or stop, think about what's going on around you and what's important. If it works for children, it will certainly work for us.

It's such a pleasure to meet some one who's comfortable being who they are. My desired outcome for this book is that many others will benefit from discovering their natural attractiveness and choosing to live their best life now. My life will never be the same. My new found freedom has set me free in more ways than I thought possible and has significantly impacted my life.

If you get just a smidgen of the freedom that I've experienced, it will be more than enough to carry you through the tough times as you continue intentional and authentic living. From my humble beginnings in Welch, West Virginia, I never could have imagined all the things that God can do for his children.

Natural attractiveness is not an exceptional circumstance. It is a state to be pursued, obtained, and shared with the world. You only have one life to live—do all that you can to enjoy it to its fullest. It's a lie from the pit of hell that life is a constant struggle and without opportunities for good belly laughs. Live your best life now and laugh often. Don't wait for permission; let the rest of the world catch up with you. Enjoy the rest of your life—after all it's the only one you have.

APPENDIX A

Clearing the Decks Checklist

- Say no to nonessential activities that you don't enjoy doing.
- Get rid of the unrealistic "to do" list that never gets done.
- Stop procrastinating and address relationship issues
- Clean out your office and make room for new business or projects
- Clear your PDA or address database of toxic people and relationships.
- Refer you high maintenance clients to business associates who have a complementary interpersonal style.
- Declutter the physical space in your home and work environment.
- Throw away outdated medicine from your cabinets
- Make time for valued relationships and activities
- Get rid of all reminders of negative life experiences.
- Have a book and software giveaway.
- Get rid of unwanted mail and email as they arrive
- Cancel subscriptions to magazines that you can't remember the last time you read them.
- Participate in scheduled exercise and keep all appointments for physicals.
- Have bills automatically drafted from your account or pay them in advance to avoid late fees.
- Don't hold grudges, freely forgive and give others the benefit of the doubt.
- Keeps a clean slate regarding your current relationships
- Arrive at least 15 minutes early for all commitments

Book and Web Resources

Chapter One – Clearing the Decks

Paul, Marilyn, *It's Hard to Make a Difference when You Can't Find Your Keys*, Viking Compass

Kustenmacher, Tiki, *How to Simplify Your Life*, McGraw-Hill Companies

Morgenstern, Julie, *Organizing from the Inside Out*, Henry Holt and Publishers, LLC

Kingston, Karen, *Clear Your Clutter with Feng Shui*, Judy Piatkus Publishers Limited

Passoff, Michelle, *Lighten Up! Free Yourself from Clutter*, Harper Collins Publishers

Jakes, T.D., *Maximize the Moment*, Berkley Publishing Group

Schechter, Harriet, *Let Go of Clutter*, McGraw-Hill

Volk, Helen D., *Beyond Clutter*, www.beyondclutter.com

Dream Cleaning and Professional Organizers, www.dreamcleaning.com

National Association of Professional Organizers, www.napo.net

Organize Now, Business & Home Office Organizing Products, www.ultoffice.com

Chapter Two – Discovering Values

Bonnstetter, Bill, *If I Knew Then What I know Now*, Forbes Custom Publishing www.ttidisc.com

Kummerow, Jean M., *New Directions in Career Planning and the Workplace*, Davies-Black Publishing

Schein, Edgar H., *Career Anchors, Discovering Your Real Values*, Pfeiffer & Company

Ellis, Dave and Lankowitz, Stan, *Human Being*, Breakthrough Enterprises, Inc.

Center for Balanced Living, www.balancedliving.com

Values Inventory, www.help-yourself.com/values

Values Grid, Discover Your Highest Values, www.sparckint.com

Chapter Three – Strengths, Talents & Skills

Buckingham, Marcus and Clifton, Donald, *Now, Discover Your Strengths*, Free Press, www.strengthsfinder.com

Covey, Stephen, *The 8th Habit, From Effectiveness to Greatness*, Free Press www.stephencovey.com

Collins, Jim, *Good To Great*, Harper Business

Gale, Linda, *Discover What You're Best At*, Fireside

Waldroop, James and Butler, Timothy, *The 12 Bad Habits that Hold Good People Back*, Currency/Doubleday

Frankel, Lois, *Overcoming Your Strengths, 8 Reasons Why Successful People Derail and How to Remain on Track*, Corporate Coaching International Publications

The Perfect Labor Storm, www.perfectlaborstorm.com

Chapter Four–Natural Attractiveness

Fortgang, Laura Berman, *Now What? 90 Days To A New Direction*, Penguin Group, Inc.

Osteen, Joel, *Live Your Best Life Now, 7 Steps to Living Your Full Potential*, Time Warner Book Group

Broder, Michael, *How to Develop Self Confidence*, Media Psychology Associates

Christian Coaching Network, www.ccn.com

International Coaching Federation, www.icf.com

Raising Your Self Esteem, www.selfesteem.org

Parikh, Jagdish, Discovering the Self: The HR Challenge

Chapter Five –Personal Mission Statements

Sher, Barbara, *Live the Life You Love*, Dell Publishing

Warren, Rick, *The Purpose Driven Life*, Zondervan

Wilkinson, Bruce, *The Dream Giver*, Multnomah Publishers

Klauser, Henriette Anne, *Write It Down, Make It Happen*, Fireside

O'Halloran, Richard and O'Halloran, David, *The Mission Primer: 4 Steps to an Effective Mission Statement*, Mission Incorporated

Jones, Laurie Beth, *The Path, Creating Your Mission Statement for Work and Life*, Hyperion

Creating a Personal Mission Statement, www.quintcareers.com

Smith, Kelly Carson, *How to make a personal mission statement*, www.digital-women.com

Franklin Covey Mission Builder, www.franklincovey.com/missionbuilder/

Chapter Six–Getting Out of My Own Way

Goulston, Mark and Goldberg, Philip, *Get Out of Your Own Way, Overcoming Self-Defeating Behavior*, Perigee Books

Shainberg, Nancy, *Getting Out of Your Own Way, Unlocking Your True Performance Potential*, CSW Luminous Press

Carson, Rick, *Taming Your Gremlin*, Quill- Harper Collins

Chapter Seven–Maintaining Natural Attractiveness

Sher, Barbara, *Live the Life You Love*, Dell Publishing

White, Jennifer, *Work Less, Make More*, John Wiley & Sons

Koch, Richard, *The 80/20 Individual*, Currency Doubleday

Closing Summary

As you come to the end of this book, it is my hope that you are well on your way to discovering and using your natural attractiveness to achieve your life's purpose. Remember, working with who you are is a lifetime activity. Every new level of self awareness creates a new opportunity to share more of yourself with those around you. It is true, just like wine, we get better with time. *Thank God for the gift of time—use it wisely.*

About the Author

Denise Brown is a wife, mother, attorney, minister, coach, author and owner of **Legal Direction** and **Timely Direction** (www.4realdirection.com) based in Louisville, Kentucky. **Legal Direction** provides balanced counsel to families and businesses enabling them to leverage the legal environment to reach their desired outcomes.

Timely Direction is a coaching, speaking and leadership development company that helps individuals reach their full potential by maximizing their strengths, talents and abilities.

Denise has practiced law for over 19 years and has over 10 years of human resource management experience in Fortune 200 corporations and as Executive Director of the Louisville and Jefferson County Human Relations Commission.

Denise regularly speaks to groups throughout the United States on leadership development and *"Working With Who You Are."* For availability, email her at denise@4realdirection.com.